THE MAN JESUS

The Man
JESUS

by GEORGE BICHLMAIR, S.J.

Translated from the German
by MARY HORGAN, B.A.

THE NEWMAN PRESS
WESTMINSTER, MARYLAND
1953

Nihil Obstat: E. A. Cerny, S.S.
      Censor Librorum

Imprimatur: Francis P. Keough, D.D.
      Archbishop of Baltimore

July 6, 1953

> The *nihil obstat* and *imprimatur* are official declarations that a book or pamphlet is free of doctrinal and moral error. No implication is contained therein that those who have granted the *nihil obstat* and *imprimatur* agree with the opinions expressed.

Contents

◇◇

Author's Preface

Within the last decade a number of excellent books on Christ have appeared, all with the same end in view: the emphasizing of the unique greatness and interior riches of the personality of the God-man.

The Son of God took human nature as a man, and we see the beauty and riches of his human nature in all their fullness—in so far as this is humanly possible—only if we also take into account the typically masculine characteristics of that nature. They are present, and more numerous than one might at first suspect. That is what I wished to point out, since it is only thus that the complete picture of the character of Christ emerges in a new lovableness.

Vienna, 30th May, 1945, the day of my return from an enforced exile lasting five and a half years.

Preface

"AFTER ME THERE COMETH A MAN . . ."

The Baptist preached in the desert of Judea and in the country around the Jordan. People gathered from all quarters to hear his words. It was a motley gathering: there were farmers and fishermen, tax-gatherers and soldiers, priests and levites, Pharisees and Sadducees.

What was it that enticed the multitude into the distant Jordan country? Certainly not the play of the reed in the wind. Neither was it curiosity to see a display of pomp from one of the rich and mighty ones of this world, a "man in soft garments," who with his train had en- *Luke* camped in the district. No! It was nothing of a worldly *vii. 24* nature that drew people into this desert region. Something of a religious nature was happening there. John was looked on as a prophet, and a prophet had not been seen in Israel for quite a long time. And even the outward appearance of this man reminded one of the prophets of old, for he wore a "garment of camel's hair, and a leathern girdle about his loins, and his meal was locusts and wild honey." That made a deep impression. People *Matt.* were reminded of Elias or Jeremias, whose appearance *iii. 4* had conveyed a like earnestness and severity. Moreover, the belief was common among the Jews that Elias would return to the earth at the end of time, immediately before the arrival of the Messias. What, then, more natural than that they should take the desert-preacher for Elias, or for the mighty prophet who was to come at the end of time! Or was he perhaps the Messias himself?

But John indignantly refuted all these suppositions about his identity. "Who art thou?" He confessed: "I am not the Christ." And when the messengers of the Jews insisted on getting an answer to their question, he insists that he is but "a voice crying in the wilderness."

John i 19ff.

John preached not himself, but another, a greater than he, who would come after him, and to the charm of whose personality he himself had already succumbed, the Messias. Long before his loving eyes had singled Jesus out from among his listeners, long before the Messias had come to ask for baptism, the image of the Master was powerfully graven on the heart of the Baptist. And picturesque and powerful images overflow into his speech as he seeks to depict for his audience the appearance of the Messias. He is the farmer "whose fan is in his hand, and he will thoroughly cleanse his floor." Or again, he likens him to a gardener, who with inexorable determination inspects the productivity of his fruit trees. Or he is the powerful king, for whose coming John, acting as herald and precursor, bids the people to prepare the way.

The Baptist, in spirit, recognized and accepted the coming Messias as a great and powerful man. He was impressed by the manliness of the Messianic figure, all the more so perhaps, because he himself was such an outstandingly masculine personality. The man John had no difficulty in finding his way to the Man Jesus. His portrait of Christ was drawn in bold, simple, severe lines. The farmer, the gardener, the governor, the judge, furnished him with his comparisons and with purely masculine forms, occupations, and activities. And the last prophet of the Old Testament speaks exactly the language of his predecessors. For all these mighty men of old confess with John: "After us there cometh a man mightier than we." And they, too, visualize and depict the future Messias as an outstanding manly figure, rather than in a vague, indeterminate way as a human being. The activity which they attribute to him is definitely masculine; that of redeeming, and liberating, bearing the burden of sinful mankind, fighting and conquering, teaching and guiding, judging and deciding, building and founding, ruling and governing. And even when they attribute to him the qualities of goodness and mildness, it is the goodness and mildness of a man who, his strength and severity notwithstanding, does not crush the weak, break the bruised reed nor quench the smoking flax.

The goodness of God has revealed itself not in graceful, tender womanhood, but in strong, vigorous manhood, thus corresponding to the Divine Wisdom, which, at once mild and virogous, rules the universe. As man the Son of God came into the world. Being man presumes the possession of definite qualities, tendencies, capacities and characteristics which originate from the Creator, and which the man is obliged to develop if he would perfectly fulfil God's design for him. This Jesus did *par excellence*. In perfect and unsurpassably glorious manhood he stands before us. One must only be able to see it to be edified and rejoice in it.

The fact that hitherto Christ has been so rarely considered as man may be partly attributed to a certain reluctance to assign to him a particular sex, thereby detracting from the universality of his personality and the richness of his human nature. But the simple truth remains, that the Son of God once became a man, and as such he is linked with man by a decided similarity, a particular stamp, where woman cannot meet him. And this is not without special significance, and there is no reason why we should not give it the fullest consideration.

Christian art, too, especially of the last two centuries, is largely responsible for the lack of emphasis on the masculine side of the character of Jesus. Pictures and images of Christ failed to portray the vigorous and manly aspect of the God-man, and pious, graceful, edifying, but weak, effeminate and sentimental caricatures of the real Christ found their way into every department of Christian life. But, apart from notable exceptions, we seek in vain for representations in which the Messias is depicted as a strong, manly figure.

There is, perhaps, a deeper reason why the image of Christ as man largely disappeared from the horizon of the Christian world during the last two centuries. The Christ cult during these centuries received great impetus through women. Devotion to the Sacred Heart in its modern form owes its first impulse to the private revelations granted by God to a woman. Likewise the dedication of the world to the Sacred Heart was first suggested by a nun, and for the establishment of the feast of Christ the King a woman labored long and earnestly, only learning on her death bed of the success of her efforts. Undoubtedly devotion to the Sacred Heart, with its accompanying idea of reparation for sin, gave plenty of scope for solid masculine piety, but it was adopted predominantly by women and unconsciously given a feminine twist.

Naturally it is not our intention to question the wisdom of Divine Providence. Why should the Church, directed by the Holy Ghost, not adopt suggestions from women? Let us not regret that devotion to Christ is so largely practiced by women. What is to be regretted is that men have had so little interest in it. The grace of God addresses itself to every heart that is open and ready to receive it, but there have obviously been too few men during the last centuries whom the grace of God could use as instruments to give the newly-blossoming devotion to Christ an effective masculine stamp. Men have not sufficiently sought Christ, and, therefore, the image of Jesus as man was neglected. The woman's approach to Christ is other than the man's. She perceives and portrays the interior life of the Savior, naturally in a feminine way, softer, more sensitive, and milder than the man. And when the Christ-cult had once taken on the feminine tone, this interpretation soon found its way into the pulpit and public devotions, into prayer books and pious books. Finally the man felt out of place in the spiritual life of the Church. He withdrew, and left it for the most part to the woman.

Hence it is of supreme importance to observe the peculiar characteristics of masculine piety, and to build up a prototype of manly piety and spirituality. For the man must feel himself addressed as man in the Church, from the pulpit, in prayer book and book of devotion. How much that is awry, unjust, untrue and unmanly must in the course of time have found its way into the practical presentation of Christianity to give rise to the opinion that religion is an affair for women and most unsuitable for men.

And yet when we examine the matter more closely we find many arguments for the contrary opinion. That is true, at least, of the Catholic exposition of Christianity. Consider, for instance, the tense, severe, objective and impersonal tone of the liturgical texts. Their primary appeal is to the intellect rather than to feeling and emotion. The Christian religion was founded by a man, therefore, why should it not be a man's concern? Twelve men were the first co-workers of the Man Jesus. It was men he appointed as the pillars of his Church. It was men he called to the priesthood, and to be the dispensers of his Sacraments. Men were the first standard-bearers in his Kingdom and to man are reserved the first places in the Church.

To be a Christian means to be in living intercourse with the personal Christ. Admittedly, he is a divine person, and therefore, intercourse with him can only be through religion. But he was also truly man, and as man he proved and made good his human nature. And how well and how nobly he did so! For in Jesus, the Creator himself lived as man, and consequently he is the living, concrete protoype of the noblest, finest and fullest manhood possible. In Jesus man finds his direct model. That is not only a great grace, but an equally great privilege for the masculine sex. And by whom should the Man Jesus be better understood than by those of his own sex? Does not the human-masculine nature of the God-Man act as a wide-open door inviting men to enter? May no man henceforth heedlessly and indifferently pass by that open door!

THE MAN JESUS

CHAPTER I

The Man of Nazareth

I. THE NAME

"After eight days were accomplished that the child should be circumcised, his name was called Jesus." With these words the Evangelist describes the simple ceremony in which the child, whose birth in the stable at Bethlehem he had already recorded, received his name. He was called Jesus. With this command the Angel Gabriel had come to Mary at the Annunciation in Nazareth. "Behold thou shalt conceive in thy womb, and shall bring forth a son; and thou shalt call his name Jesus." In like manner he spoke in a dream to Joseph who doubted whether he should take Mary to wife; "Joseph, son of David, fear not to take unto thee Mary thy wife, for that which is conceived in her is of the Holy Ghost. And she shall bring forth a son: and thou shalt call his name Jesus. For he shall save his people from their sins." *Luke i. 31* *Matt. i. 20f.*

The giving of the name Jesus was therefore in obedience to a divine command. God himself chose it from all the customary human names. By the Incarnation the Son of God appeared on the human stage and made his entry into history; therefore he had to have a name to distinguish and differentiate him from other men. So he was called Jesus.

I

The divine origin of this name and the historical uniqueness of him who bore it would lead us to believe that the name itself was extraordinary and not in general use in Israel. But it is not so. The name Jesus or Josue was, until the beginning of the second century A.D., very widely used among the Jews. Beginning from Josue, who succeeded Moses as the leader of the Chosen People, until Jesus surnamed Justus, a co-worker of the Apostle Paul, we meet in Holy Scripture with not a few who bore this name. In the genealogy of Jesus, as Luke gives it to us, the name Jesus occurs once, and Flavius Josephus mentions about twenty persons of the name, ten of whom were contemporaries of Jesus, so that this name was by no means unusual or uncommon among the people to whom Jesus belonged. The Son of God who would become "like us in all things" became like us also in that he took an ordinary widely-used human name, and by so doing really made himself one with his people. "Jesus" was a decidedly masculine name. We do not read that a woman ever bore it.

This name must, however, have a special significance; otherwise it would be unintelligible why it was bestowed under the express command of God. In what does the unusualness, the divinity of this name consist? Not in the sound but in the depth and meaning of its content. "The name signifies the greatness of His Majesty," says St. Bernard, "for this Jesus does not, like so many of His predecessors, bear an empty and insignificant name. His great name is no image but a reality." The original idea in giving a name was actually to mark the individuality of the bearer by a characteristic sign. Thus may Adam have called the animals in his immediate neighborhood by exterior appellations. In later times the conferring of names may have become more arbitrary, but the name always remained the distinguishing mark of the individual, and so there arose a mutual interchangeability between the name and the person who bore it.

To exterminate the name means to annihilate its owner; to enter the name into the Book of Life is synonymous with the admission of the person into the messianic kingdom, and to blot out the name signifies damnation. A change of name should be marked by an important change in the circumstances of a life. Thus, the oriental kings changed their names on their accession to the throne. God himself changed the name of Abram to Abraham, Jacob to Israel. In the Kingdom of God the servants of the Master will be known by new names; the new Sion itself will receive a new designation. In Holy Scripture the bestowal of a name has a far deeper significance than might appear to us.

In the first place, God undertakes nothing meaningless or indifferent. If He Himself chose the name for the future man, Jesus, He obviously wished thereby to give expression to something important and definitive. In actual fact there is something divinely great and genial in this name. It is the simplest, and yet the most perfect and most pregnant expression of that which he who bore it was: Salvation, Help from God, and indeed Salvation and Help simply and essentially in fullness, in power, in strength and in sublimity. His whole incarnate Being and activity was "Jesus," that is, Salvation and Help from God. In Jesus God came to men as the most effective help, as determined Redeemer, as powerful Savior, as manly Executor of the mighty work of the redemption of men. And so this man, at the end of his life, could pray to his heavenly Father: "I have finished the work which thou gavest me to do." "And therefore, this name has not been given to him, but inherited by him, not an image, but a reality" (St. Bernard). "Thou shalt call his name Jesus, for he shall save his people from their sins. He

Luke i. 51

Luke i. 30f.

shall be great, and shall be called the Son of the Most High . . . he shall reign . . . and of his Kingdom there shall be no end." What truth lies hidden in the content, what riches in the person, what a wealth of power and majesty attaches to this name. No mere human historical personage ever justified his name as did the Man of Nazareth.

What a noble manly figure should rise up before our mind's eye as often as we speak or hear spoken the name of Jesus! It should endorse the words of St. Bernard in praise of this name: "a person is refreshed every time he remembers it, new power is given to the understanding of him who thinks on it, that through it the over-wrought mind is re-animated, moral strength renewed, good and upright habits are maintained and chaste affections called forth." Unfortunately this is not true of many present-day Christians. The name of Jesus has lost its resonance, and in many hearts it awakens no more than a faint religious memory, or calls to mind only the picture of a soft, mild Savior, an image of weary forbearance robbed of all divinely triumphant strength, with expressionless eyes and weak, sensual mouth, infinitely removed from the sharply-defined, firmly-stamped features of the Man Jesus.

The name which Jesus bears is, in the first place, an expression of His manhood. In order to appreciate it properly, it should summon for us some of that local color and timbre with which the inhabitants of Nazareth spoke and heard it. But for this we lack the essential cultural and language associations. For us the name of Jesus is primarily a religious, a sacred name. As such it has an intonation and a meaning independent of the mother-earth from which it sprang. But it is just in this interpretation that it loses much of its powerful resonance, for it is frequently abused and blasphemed and thoughtlessly uttered. And that quite contrary to the mind of the Church! For if she has enriched with many indulgences the "devout invocation of the holy Name of Jesus," it is in order thereby to direct the attention of the faithful to the person of the Man and Redeemer, Jesus Christ. She is not concerned with the mere sound of the name but with the person who hears it. It is the Master himself we should call to mind when we invoke his name. This applies also to the Catholic greeting: "Praised be Jesus Christ!" If these words do not evoke, even for a fleeting instant, the divinely majestic figure of the Man of Nazareth before our gaze they remain mere sound and smoke.

A goodly number of indulgences and other prayers open with the words: "Sweetest Jesus . . ." There is even an ecclesiastically * approved "Litany of the Sweetest Name of Jesus," and a hymn beginning with the words, "O sweetest of all Names" is very commonly sung. Have not such expressions contributed to the softening and sentimentalizing of the name of Jesus, and thus—let us say it quite openly—caused men to lose the taste for it? This may be, but it is due to a misinterpretation of the original meaning of the words, for in the above expression "sweet" and "sweetest" is a translation of the Latin *"dulcissime Jesu."* In its original significance this word smacks not in the least of sentimentality. It applies to the whole person and means rather "loving," or "friendly" or "well disposed." When applied to a human being it excludes all offensiveness, hardness or indifference. The *dulcis* Jesus gains in amiability by the attribution, and it ensures that his powerful masculine Being has in it nothing repelling, rough or terrifying.

The name Jesus should call to our mind the Man of Nazareth, the young man who, when in the company of

* Local.

his comrades, raised his head attentively, questioningly, when a voice from somewhere called "Jesus," and the man to whom Philip referred, when, following on his first encounter with Jesus, he told Nathanael: "We have found him of whom Moses in the law and the prophets did write, Jesus the son of Joseph of Nazareth." It should remind us of the mighty wonder-worker, whom Peter had in mind, when he called out to the lame man at the gate of the temple: "In the name of Jesus Christ of Nazareth, arise, and walk," and of the supernatural greatness and superiority over all men, to which Paul testified: "God hath exalted him, and hath given him a name which is above all names: That in the name of Jesus every knee should bow, of those that are in heaven, on earth, and under the earth: And every tongue should confess that the Lord Jesus Christ is in the glory of God the Father."

*John
i. 45*

*Acts
iii. 6*

*Phil.
ii. 9f.*

2. THE CARPENTER

While Jesus was assisting at the Feast of Tabernacles, and the Jewish authorities were already busy with plans to bring about his death, he was the subject of much talk in the town. Among other things people said: "Is not this he whom they seek to kill? And behold he speaketh openly, and they say nothing to him. Have the rulers known for a truth that this is the Christ? But we know this man whence he is: but when the Christ cometh, no man knoweth whence he is."

*John
vii. 25ff.*

It was known generally whence Jesus came. To differentiate between him and others who bore the name, he was called "Jesus of Nazareth in Galilee," or "Jesus of Nazareth," or simply "The Nazarene." Nazareth was his home-town; that was generally known.

In the little town of Nazareth itself he was spoken of as the "Son of Joseph," the "Son of the carpenter," the

"Carpenter," the "Son of Mary," the "Brother of James, Joseph, Judas and Simon." He did not stand out in any way beyond the other men of the place, and like them he was known only by his trade or by his origin. It was only when he emerged from the restricted circle of his life as a tradesman, and began his public mission that people were surprised and began to ask one another in astonishment: "How did he come by this wisdom, and these strange powers? Is not this the carpenter's son, whose mother is called Mary, and his brethren James and Joseph and Simon and Judas? And do not his sisters, all of them, live near us? How is it that all this has come to him?" This astonishment on the part of his hearers shows us clearly that hitherto Jesus had attracted very little attention; that he was very much a man among men, and a tradesman among tradesmen. Nobody observed or suspected anything unusual in him.

Matt. xiii. 55

And so it is that we must picture him to ourselves: as an ordinary working-man, with calloused hands and furrowed, sunburnt features, dressed like his fellow-workers, practicing the manners and customs of the district, speaking the rough Galilean dialect, and immediately recognizable to every stranger as a Galilean, as was Peter in the courtyard of Caiphas.

In the beginning Jesus practiced as a carpenter with his foster-father Joseph, and after the death of Joseph he must have taken over and carried on alone. In Palestine almost everything that was made of wood, or in the construction of which wood was used, belonged to the trade of the carpenter: the dressing of the great beams which supported the house, and of the little staves and rods which served as a hold for straw, doors and wooden bolts, the primitive furniture, as well as ploughs and other agricultural implements. The carpenter was bricklayer, coach-builder, and joiner all in one. If a field were attached to the house, whether as private property or held on lease, as was probably the case in Mary's household, the carpenter was responsible for its care and cultivation.

The Man Jesus showed familiarity with all these various kinds of work. He understood the good and bad soil on which a house may be built; he speaks of doors and corner-stones and foundation-walls, yea! even of the estimate which a man must make beforehand if he contemplates building a tower. He knows of the mustard-*Mark* seed which is set in the garden: "Which when it is sown *iv. 31 ff.* in the earth is less than all the seeds that are in the earth. And when it is sown, it groweth up and becometh greater than all herbs, and shooteth out great branches, so that the birds of the air may dwell under the shadow thereof." He speaks of work in the field as one who knows it, not merely from hearsay nor as a mere onlooker, but from personal experience, even as one who has watched, with love and interest, the many mysterious little events which take place there. He is familiar with the scattering of the seed, and the quality of the soil on which the seed may fall. He has seen the birds follow in the wake of the sower, and pick up the corn which fell beside the path. He knows exactly the fate of the seed which falls on *Mark* stony ground where it finds very little soil: "and it shot *iv. 2 ff.* up immediately because it had no depth of earth. And when the sun was risen, it was scorched, and because it had no root, it withered away." The humility of one speaking of the soil, but at the same time confidence in the trustworthiness of nature, and the joy of the 'expectant farmer speak from the words in which he describes the growth and maturing of the seed: "the seed should spring and grow up whilst he knoweth not. For the earth of itself bringeth forth fruit, first the blade, then the ear, afterwards the full corn in the ear. And when the fruit is brought forth, immediately he putteth *Mark iv. 26ff.* in the sickle, because the harvest is come."

He who can describe the sprouting and ripening of the seed with such tenderness and delicacy must have known suspense for the fate of his own seed, and rejoiced over its fruitfulness. As a man familiar with domestic and agricultural work alike, Jesus knows too what is becoming and unbecoming in a farmworker; when he comes home from the field he may not immediately take his place at table, but he must first serve his master. And the tasks of the vineyard are not unknown to him. He understands the laying out of a vineyard and knows the daily wage of a worker. As a farmer he is accustomed to observing the weather. One can almost hear him there among his neighbors in the quiet evening hour discussing the weather forecast for the following day: "It is fair weather, the sky is red." Or, as in the morning he hurries to the field with his sickle and calls a warning to the passers-by: "There will be a storm today, the sky is red and lowering."

That is Jesus of Nazareth: a man who works constantly, hard, indefatigably, a man of the soil, a lover of nature, simple in his dress and way of life, outwardly in no way different from other men of his calling and native-place, whom he had become like in all things "sin *Hebrews iv. 15* excepted."

The evangelists give no details of the years spent by Jesus as a carpenter in Nazareth. Apart from the pilgrimage of the twelve-year-old youth to Jerusalem, there are two short, generally accepted remarks which give us some insight into this period. Of the Child Jesus we read: "The Child grew and waxed strong, full of wisdom, and the grace of God was in him." And of the *Luke ii. 40* young Man Jesus we are told: "He went down with them, and came to Nazareth, and was subject to them"

Luke . . . "Jesus advanced in wisdom and age, and grace with
ii. 51 God and men."

No mention is made of any disturbances or crises during the childhood, youth or early manhood of Jesus. On
the contrary, from the scantiness of the information
which has come down to us concerning these years we
may deduce that they were years of harmonious development and flourishing prosperity. "The Child grew and
waxed strong." We are not told that Jesus was ill at any
time. But the extraordinary physical efforts which he
made during his public mission would lead us to conclude that he enjoyed a thoroughly sound and healthy
constitution. "He advanced in wisdom and age." He
was no infant prodigy who might have caused a sensation; neither was he a precocious nor a backward child.
He found favor with God because of his fresh, sound
piety, and with men because of his friendly ways. The
young man found the bridge to his fellow-men. Courageously and self-confidently he grew into his environment and the society of his fellow-men. He was no
solitary, no oddity, no misanthropist, no fanatic, no
enthusiast for any strange or exaggerated aim. His un-
questioning obedience to his parents testifies to that. He
knew how to give way discreetly without thereby forfeit-
ing his manliness or his interior independence.

3. THE TRAVELLING PREACHER

During his public mission Jesus once visited his native
town of Nazareth, a visit which St. Luke describes in
detail in the fourth chapter of his Gospel. This account
shows clearly the great change which took place when
Jesus left the intimacy of his home and devoted himself
to the life of a wandering preacher. It affords us also an
interesting insight into the flood of conflicting opinions,
feelings and emotions let loose when he re-appeared

among the people of his native town in a new and un-
expected role.

That first departure of Jesus from Nazareth was very
probably quite unspectacular. His intention was to seek
out the great preacher of penance, who was preaching
around the lower Jordan. There was nothing remarkable in that. Other men of Galilee had done likewise,
as, for instance, the brothers Peter and Andrew from
Capharnaum and John of Bethsaida, and very many
others.

For some time the absence of Jesus may have passed
unnoticed. Nobody bothered very much about his com-
ings and goings. Gradually, however, rumors began to
spread that Jesus was preaching in the same district as
John. At first, this was, perhaps, not taken very seriously,
but soon the news began to seep through that he was
doing rather extraordinary things. He was supposed to
have changed water into wine at a marriage feast in
Cana. In Capharnaum he had cured the sick son of a
ruler. Pilgrims reported "the things he had done at Jeru- *John*
salem on the festival day." It was all rather disconcert- *iv. 45*
ing, to say the least of it! Gradually, then, his behavior
became more and more the general topic of conversation
in Nazareth. "The fame of him went out through the
whole country, and he taught in their synagogues, and
was magnified by all." That made them prick up their *Luke*
ears. Their curiosity knew no bounds. And then one day *iv. 14f.*
came the startling news: "He is coming to Nazareth."
We can appreciate the tension with which the Nazarenes
awaited his arrival. And then he was there!

Let us leave Luke to describe the manner of his coming: "He went into the synagogue according to his custom on the Sabbath-day, and he rose up to read." There
was nothing unusual in that. Every Jewish man at that *Luke*
time still had the right to read a passage from the Scrip- *iv. 16ff.*

ture during divine worship, and to comment on what he had read. He signified his willingness to read by standing up, and then he was called forward by the synagogue attendant. In the synagogue at Nazareth it probably did not often happen that a member of the congregation announced his intention of reading, for, as a general rule, this duty fell to the lot of men more or less officially appointed for the task. But on the Sabbath-day that Jesus was present, everybody would have expected him to read and speak, especially as it was known that it was his custom to do so in other synagogues. He was handed the Book of Isaias. He unrolled it, and read the passage: *Isaias* "The spirit of the Lord is upon me, wherefore, he hath *lxi. 1f.* anointed me, to preach the Gospel to the poor; he hath sent me, to heal the contrite of heart, to preach deliverance to the captives, and sight to the blind, to set at liberty them that are bruised, and to preach the acceptable year of the Lord." Then he closed the book, handed it to the attendant, and sat down. All eyes were fixed upon him in tense expectation. And he began to speak: "This day is fulfilled this Scripture in your ears."

The evangelist does not record for us the remainder of his sermon. But Jesus must have spoken eloquently, for "all gave testimony to him, and they wondered at the words of grace that proceeded from his mouth, and they said: Is not this the Son of Joseph?" Their first reaction may have been one of honest delight that one of themselves, from their own unpretentious little town, could speak so eloquently and convincingly. And that it should be the retiring carpenter of all men! Who would have expected it of him!

But soon their mood changed. It gradually sank in that the carpenter was actually claiming to be something extraordinary, a messenger of God, a prophet! Perhaps he was even under the delusion that he was the Messias!

At first they took this astounding thing calmly, because they were still spellbound by the magic of his words, and the powerful influence of his person. And they fully expected him to repeat in his native town such wonders as he had wrought in Capharnaum and elsewhere. But he refused to do so. And their disappointment was great. Their curiosity must remain unsatisfied. The argument which he advanced in explanation of his refusal exasperated them still more. "Amen I say to you, that no prophet is accepted in his own country." So he really would have them believe he was a prophet! Why, he even would put himself on a level with Elias and Eliseus and apparently expressed himself contemptuously about Israel, as if God preferred the heathen to his own chosen people. That was too much! Disappointment and embitterment grew apace. They were utterly carried away by the violence of their passions: envy, jealousy, hatred, anger, rage! "They rose up and thrust him out of the city; and they brought him to the brow of the hill, whereupon their city was built, that they might cast him down headlong. But he passing through the midst of them, went his way." What a splendid, what a majestic exit that was! This man knew what he wanted, and he was able to achieve what he wanted. *Luke iv. 29f.*

The carpenter had now become a genuine Rabbi, and he wore the appropriate costume. The Palestinian teachers of the law bore this title. The expression "Rab" meant something like "great" or "mighty," and "Rabbi" might be interpreted as "my Lord," or "my Master," or "my Teacher." Originally a rarely used, highly respectful form of address by scholars, it had developed gradually into a common form of address, into a title from which the "my" was omitted, something as the "Mon" is to-day in the French title "Monsieur."

From the very beginning this title was applied to Jesus

quite spontaneously. Everybody addressed him as Rabbi, the Apostles and disciples, the common people, the distinguished hosts who occasionally invited him to their tables. Even the Scribes and Pharisees dared not deny him this mark of deference. With the words "Hail, Rabbi," the traitor Judas betrayed his Master into the hands of the enemy. And Jesus himself admitted his claim to the title, and the profession indicated by it, as is shown clearly by his words to the Apostles after the Last Supper: "You call me Master, and Lord," he said to them, "and you say well, for so I am. If then I, being *your* Lord and Master, have washed your feet; you also ought to wash one another's feet." It would seem that the people occasionally addressed the Apostles also with this title, but that Jesus would not tolerate. "Be not you called Rabbi," he admonishes them, for one is your *Matt.* Master, and all you are brethren . . . Neither be ye *xxiii. 8* called masters, for one is your master, Christ."

He would have it clearly understood, at the same time, that he was not a colleague of the professional Rabbis, the Scribes and Pharisees, and in the most decided manner he denied any connection with him. He considered them too arrogant and conceited. For everybody knew that they chose the places of honor at banquets, and the first places in the synagogues, that they wished to be saluted in public and be called "Rabbi" by the people. Such conduct was utterly repulsive to his modest nature and manly honesty.

The title and profession of Rabbi was confined to men; women were absolutely excluded from the ranks of the Rabbis. In Israel a woman was forbidden to study the law, let alone to define or teach it in public. As Rabbi, then, Jesus deliberately placed himself among the men of his people and claimed his prerogatives as such.

His public appearance made a tremendous impression.

"Never did man speak like this man." So said the messengers whom the Pharisees had sent to apprehend him. They did not seize him, because they were themselves taken captive by him. Again and again the evangelists record the cries of astonishment which burst from the listening crowds. "He teaches as one having authority." "People were astonished at his doctrine. For he was teaching them as one having power, and not as the scribes." "They were astonished at his doctrine, for his speech was with power." Even the Scribes once were forced to testify to his greatness: "Master, thou hast said well." For something new and mysterious spoke from the lips of this man.

John vii. 46

Mark vii. 28

i. 22

Luke iv. 32

Luke xx. 39

What was it that was new and striking in his utterances? What differentiated his way of teaching from that of the Scribes and Pharisees? Let us for a moment disregard the content of his doctrine, and consider only the external form and style of his delivery, which was found to be quite different from that of the professional Rabbis, so different, in fact, that it admitted of no comparison. Jesus practiced the profession of Rabbi, despite the fact that he had not studied in any of the recognized schools. "How doth this man know letters, having never learned," so the professional Rabbis asked one another. Soon it must have become obvious to the ordinary people that his method of teaching did not conform to that of any of the recognized schools. He did not adopt, or feel at home in any of the accepted school jargon. Nor was he content with quoting the views and assertions of earlier teachers of the law, and then elaborating and annotating them from his own erudition. His was no mere bookish learning and mechanical knowledge of the law. Not learning, but Wisdom! Such unheard-of practical philosophy, such assurance and conviction, such manifestation of piety and holiness as one can only admire, but not attempt to

John vii. 15

explain came forth from him. He gave the impression of one who not only *knew* but *saw*, of one who was giving testimony, not of another, but of himself. On first hearing him one might be pardoned for thinking it was merely the carpenter of Nazareth who was speaking, so simple and unpretentious were his words, so clear and logical his expositions, so spontaneously did he express himself; but on closer attention and meditation one felt that each of his thoughts and utterances held unsuspected depths of meaning, and revealed further mysterious associations hitherto untouched by man.

In a general survey we may distinguish three distinct fields of action wherein Jesus principally carried out his work of teaching. On the Sabbath-days his custom was to teach in the synagogues at the conclusion of the Scriptural readings, as Luke has recorded of his visit to Nazareth. On such occasions his discourses were very probably of the nature of edifying, moralizing sermons. Frequently he taught in the open. It was then that he delivered his parables on the Kingdom of God, his favorite theme, it might be called. Then there flowed from his lips those glorious similes, for which surrounding nature often provided the inspiration. He loved the mountains and hills especially for his teaching purposes. From this vantage ground the dwellings of men far below, with their innumerable daily distractions and trivial cares, seemed dim and distant, insignificant and unimportant, by contast with the weighty truths and mighty deeds which he proclaimed. Mountains and elevations, the lake of Galilee spread out before them, or the wide expanse of plain formed a suitable framework for the new spiritual vistas which he was opening up before his audience. And so Matthew introduces the Sermon on the Mount: "Seeing the multitudes, he went up into a mountain, and when he was set down, his disciples

came unto him, and opening his mouth he taught them, *Matt.*
saying: Blessed are the poor in spirit . . ." What *v. 1ff.*
glorious harmony of message and environment, of nature
and revelation, of earthly and heavenly kingdom! For
such effects the Man Jesus possessed a fine sensibility!

To be sure there was no place and no occasion which
Jesus would not have used for the promulgation of his
doctrine. He taught and preached wherever he found
hearts needy and ready to receive his words: in his
restricted quarters in Capharnaum, in the boat on the
Sea of Galilee, in cities and towns, from couches at the
tables of his hosts, in the porches of the temple in Jerusalem, before great crowds and in the intimacy of private
conversations, to inquiring visitors, and in so-called
chance encounters. But whatever the circumstances, he
invariably aroused admiration by his mysterious, determined, assured personality. A power went forth from
him. Not only a miraculous power, but the power of his
perfect manhood, his nobility of mind, the fullness of his
interior riches. Who does not experience, even to-day, a
burning longing to hear once more the firm and yet mild,
the clear and yet ardent tones of his manly voice!

With what inward emotion must this man have pronounced the glorious Beatitudes! And how annihilating
sound the sentences which fall like a lightning-flash as a
sevenfold threat of woe on the heads of the Scribes and
Pharisees! How the magic and charm of his words must
have held the multitudes captive! How clear and thrilling his voice as he initiated his Apostles into the meaning
of the parables!

Indeed, the carpenter and Rabbi of Nazareth spoke
quite otherwise than the Scribes and Pharisees.

4. HIS MASCULINE CHARACTER

The human soul is a great and impenetrable mystery.

No one can pretend to understand how thought originates or is linked up with judgment, how free will expresses itself, what feelings and affections are aroused in a given set of circumstances, or what will be the reaction of any individual soul in this or that emergency. The individual himself is incapable of understanding clearly the movements of his own soul. How much less can he presume to penetrate and describe the mysterious workings of another soul.

The psychologist looks on it as a signal victory if he succeeds in classifying and arranging human beings according to their interior life, but the individual human soul jealously guards its secrets and mocks at categories and generalizations.

If that is true of the ordinary human being, how inexpressibly more applicable it is to the interior life of Jesus. How he felt and thought and judged and decided in all the details of his life, how all his interior movements were unified and linked up with, and subordinated to his personal decision, and how, conversely, the whole gamut of his feelings, perceptions and experiences were shaped and colored by his Divinity—all that must remain for us a mystery. It is in vain that we try to describe this inner life, this mentality, in scientific terms, or to judge it according to common human standards. It is in vain that we endeavor to assign to Jesus a particular character or temperament, or to consider his mentality under any of the usual categories, for even while we do so we are compelled to acknowledge the futility of our effort.

The more our mind tries to encompass him the more he eludes our grasp, and the richer and deeper and more unique and universal his character appears. The intellectual and spiritual life of Jesus is at once the richest and most varied, the most individual and clearly defined which the human mind can conceive.

Is it not, then, a vain and useless undertaking to wish to ascribe to Jesus a masculine character? Is it not to set a limitation to him, in contradiction of what has been said above? In the case of Jesus it is, indeed, not permissible to speak of a masculine character, in the sense of the specific, distinguishing mark of his inner life. Of that there can be no question. Jesus was more than man. In his Being the fullness of humanity was united to the fullness of the Divinity. But he was man nevertheless. His manhood constitutes the lowest plan of his Divine existence, and in virtue of the fact that he was man he had a number of specifically masculine qualities, corporal and spiritual. It is particularly interesting to observe how, in the fullness and richness of his incarnate nature, his manhood expresses itself even in his spiritual life, for he was loyal to his manhood and would not leave any aspect of God's creation undeveloped. In this attitude of his there is a singular beauty, which we shall examine and savor as we feebly attempt to determine for ourselves the peculiarly masculine traits in the character of Christ.

Where exactly should we expect to find masculine characteristics in the person of Jesus? Primarily, so it seems to us, in the objectivity and impersonality which is so obvious in his preaching and teaching as in every other activity of his. The great and important thing always was that spiritual issues should be kept well in the foreground. He never once referred to his personal feelings or experiences, or advanced them as motives for action; his constant and unvarying appeal was to the objective, fundamental principles of the moral law as laid down by God, and therefore, he appealed much more to the reason than to the emotions of his hearers.

It has been said of him that he had a pronounced "lean-
ing to the rational."

That is the really remarkable thing about the Man
Jesus: that, although his personality made such a deep
and enduring impression, and his miracles should have
directed the interest and attention of his audience exclusively to his own person, in actual fact the enthusiastic
demonstrations of the people very often transcended
his human person and were addressed immediately to
God. So powerfully did his entire Being at all times
speak of Another, of the One, Great, Omnipotent, of
God. How frequently the Gospels read: "The multitude
glorified God that gave such power to men." "All wondered and glorified God." "There came a fear upon
them all; and they glorified God saying: A great prophet
is risen up amongst us; and God hath visited his people."
On his entrance to Jerusalem the "whole multitude of
his disciples began with joy to praise God with a loud
voice, for all the mighty works they had seen."

Matt.
ix. 8

Mark
ii. 12

Luke
vii. 16

Luke
xix. 36

The Man Jesus preached God even without speaking
His name. It would appear that those who were privileged to hear him instinctively sensed that here was a
man of one ideal, one interest, one aim, one anxiety, one
joy—the glory of God, and involuntarily they were
drawn in to this orientation of his Being, his Will, and
his Work. That was the real purpose of his coming
among us. The account of the raising of Lazarus reveals
to us how he would have his miracles understood: "This
sickness is not unto death, but for the glory of God: that
the Son of God may be glorified by it." And when the
woman from the crowd blessed his Mother, and thus indirectly praised him, how hurriedly and anxiously he
turns attention away from his own person: "Yea, rather
blessed are they who hear the word of God and keep it."
Nor would he permit the man of Gerasa, from whom he

John
xi. 4

Luke
xi. 28

had cast out a legion of devils, to attach himself to him:
He dismissed him with the words: "Go into thy house to
thy friends, and tell them how great things the Lord
hath done for thee, and hath had mercy on thee." The
man "went his way, and began to publish in Decapolis
how great things Jesus had done for him." But, it may
be objected, did not Jesus actually make himself the
center of all his teaching? Did he not say to the Jews:
"You have heard . . ., but I say to you." Did he not
point to his own person as the way of salvation, the
Alpha and Omega of all religious life? And did he not
demand from his disciples that they should follow him
unconditionally? Certainly it is true that Jesus spoke of
himself as the decisive norm, the one great necessity in
men's lives, but then he was speaking primarily as the
Teacher, the Leader, the Pioneer, the Liberator, the Redeemer, in a word, it was the man in him who spoke
thus, it was his manhood already acting and illuminating
as "the image and glory of God." This point we shall
treat in more detail in a later chapter.

Mark v. 19

I Cor. xi. 7

Particularly illuminative of the character of the Man
Jesus are the parables which he used in his discourses.
The images and allegories which a person employs in his
speech reveal most clearly the peculiar stamp of his mind
and imagination, for such figures of speech have their
origin primarily in the free play of the imagination and
the moods of the spirit. Supposing this to be so, one may
dare to assert that, even if we did not know that the
parables and allegories of the Gospels came from the lips
of Jesus, we might nevertheless deduce from their
peculiar cast that they emanated from the mind of a
man, for they unmistakably portray the imagination,
mind and way of thinking of a man. It is only very
rarely, and, as it were, by way of exception that women
play a part in them, as, for instance, the woman who

sweeps out the house and finds the lost Drachmas, the widow before the judge, the woman who leavens the meal, the wise and foolish virgins. That exhausts the feminine element in the parables, and we must further add that the virgins play only a secondary role in the parable of the approaching Bridegroom, and likewise the widow before the unjust judge. In all the other parables without exception, man holds the stage. Such pictures as the workers in the vineyard, the unjust steward, the rich man and Lazarus, the good Shepherd, the good Samaritan, the prodigal son, to mention only a few of the parables and allegories in which men play the primary role could not have emanated from the mind of a woman. No! in them a man was at work, in them the creative imagination of a man unfolded itself, in them the man's conception of the world and everyday events revealed itself.

Jesus himself sums up his metaphorical discourses on the kingdom of Heaven, "every scribe instructed in the *Matt.* Kingdom of Heaven is like to a man that is a house-*xiii. 52* holder, who bringeth forth out of his treasure new things and old." In the case of Jesus, this treasure was hidden in the depth and abundance of his manly soul.

The Pharisees unconsciously furnished the shortest, most appropriate, and most beautiful testimony to the manly character of Jesus, when they approached him concerning the legality of paying tribute to the Romans, and introduced their query with the words: "Master, we know that thou art a true speaker, and carest not for any *Mark* man: for thou regardest not the person of men, but *xii. 14* teachest the way of God in truth."

Yes! that was the Man Jesus!

5. HIS MASCULINE WAY OF LIFE

Jesus must have been a man of sound health and powerful physique. This conclusion we have already drawn from the two statements with which St. Luke concludes his account of the childhood and youth of Jesus. A consideration of the kind of life which Jesus led during his public mission will confirm this conclusion, for from it we get the impression that only a man of robust health could have endured such a life.

The fact alone that he led such an arduous life of constant movement from place to place would indicate that. He traversed the whole of Palestine many times, a country of some 11,500 square miles in area, with a length of 150 miles and an average breadth of 88 miles. He had his headquarters, so to speak, in Capharnaum, but he was rarely to be found there. He would never consent to establish himself in any particular place, though the people often tried to hold him: "To other cities also I must preach the Kingdom of God; for therefore, am I sent," was his reply to them when they were unwilling to let him depart from them. He did not spare himself. *Luke iv. 43* "Being wearied with his journey" he must have seated himself to rest a little on the brink of a well or by the wayside more frequently than the one occasion expressly recorded for us in the Gospel narrative. Speaking constantly must have wearied him exceedingly, for he taught and preached for the most part in the open air and before great multitudes. One can imagine what an effort it must cost a preacher to speak in the open to an audience of more than five thousand. And the audiences which listened to Jesus must often have numbered far more. On the occasion of the first multiplication of the loaves, which concluded the discourse in the open, the number of men present was five thousand, not counting women and children. And there is not a doubt that Jesus would have taken pains to speak loudly enough to be heard and understood by the greatest number possible. And that under the blazing Palestinian sun!

Matt.
viii. 19ff.

A scribe once approached him and said to him: "Master, I will follow thee whithersoever thou shalt go." Jesus answered him: "The foxes have holes, and the birds of the air nests: but the son of man hath not where to lay his head." Consider well, he obviously wished to say to him, whether your strength is sufficient to endure the kind of life I lead! In the morning he very often must have had no idea where his midday meal was to come from, or where he should pass the night. For the most part he was dependent on the uncomfortable and inhospitable public inns, if he did not prefer to sleep under the stars. And doubtlessly he must have spent many nights under the open sky. On the whole he seems to have had a decided preference for an open-air life. That would indicate that he was hardened to the vagaries of wind and weather, and especially to the not inconsiderable fluctuations of temperature, not only between summer and winter, but also between day and night. The Man who refused to turn stones into bread, though he might have done so, never once in all his travels worked a miracle to ameliorate his lot. He loved simplicity and poverty. "Freely have you received, freely give. Do not possess gold, nor silver, nor money in your purses. Nor scrip for your journey, nor two coats, nor shoes, nor a staff!" What he enjoined on his disciples when he sent them out to preach, he himself had undoubtedly practiced before their eyes.

Matt.
x. 8ff.

All the intimate details of the daily life of Jesus during his public mission have by no means been recorded for us; the rare hints that have come down to us were related by chance and incidental to events of major importance. Thus, for example we are told in the Gospel of St. Mark: "And rising very early, going out he went into a desert place: and there prayed." Simon and his companions followed him, and, having found him, they said

Mark
i. 35

to him: "All seek for thee." Another time—it was on the
occasion of the first multiplication of the loaves—we
read that in the evening after a busy day he told his
disciples to cross the lake. He himself dismissed the
people and "went into a mountain alone to pray." St.
Luke introduces his account of the choosing of the
twelve Apostles with the words: "In those days he went
into a mountain to pray, and he passed the whole night
in the prayer of God. And when day was come, he called
unto him his disciples: and he chose twelve of them
whom also he named Apostles." Nor did the following
day bring him any respite. It was rarely that he allowed
himself any recreation, and if, in consideration for his
disciples, he decided to relax a little he at once relin-
quished the idea when he noticed that the people wished
to approach him. In this connection the events related
by St. Mark in the sixth chapter of his Gospel are significant: "And the Apostles coming together unto Jesus,
related to him all things that they had done and taught.
And he said to them: Come apart into a desert place,
and rest a little. For there were many coming and going:
and they had not so much as time to eat. And going up
into a ship, they went into a desert place apart. And they
saw them going away, and many knew: and they ran
flocking thither on foot from all the cities, and were
there before them. And Jesus going out saw a great
multitude: and he had compassion on them, because
they were as sheep not having a shepherd, and he began
to teach them many things."

How very seldom he got a little time to himself during
the day! The people constantly crowded around him
and were witnesses to his every movement. What a tremendous mental effort it required to endure such crowds
daily, hourly, for weeks and months on end! And they
always wanted something from him; he was constantly

*Matt.
xiii. 23*

*Luke
vi. 12*

*Mark
vi. 30f.*

engaged in helping and healing, in teaching, explaining and consoling, in giving and suffering, while he himself had nobody in whom he could confide, or who would have really understood him. In truth this man knew what it means to stand, to walk, to suffer in interior loneliness. In this he was really and truly man. To be man meant, for him, no mere prerogative over the weaker sex, but a sacred obligation to teach and to guide, to endure and to support, to work and to worry.

Matt.
xi. 28
"Come to me all you that labour, and are burdened, and I will refresh you." In this great, superhuman invitation we find the complete expression of the unique and solitary Man of Nazareth.

CHAPTER II

The Man in Pursuit
of His Mission

I. UNWEARIED BY LONG WAITING

Every normal human being carries within his soul the elementary need to exist for something or somebody. He wants to see a meaning in his life and a purpose in his activities. The man who considers his life meaningless and purposeless and regards himself as superfluous in the world, loses the will to live, and the temptation to put a violent end to his life becomes almost overpowering. Those who have wearied of life, and they who have been snatched from the jaws of suicidal death have testified to the truth of this assertion.

There is a marked difference between the masculine and feminine conception of a complete and purposeful life. In the woman's nature the need predominates to exist for somebody, to care for somebody, to devote herself to somebody's service; whereas, the man experiences rather the urge to live and to spend himself for a great mission or achievement, but in the case of both sexes the ultimate end is the same, namely the need for an absorbing vocation in life.

We believe that we are not wrong, or that we do not depreciate the person of Jesus, when we say that the Man Jesus must have experienced a similar need. He, too, felt the urge to occupy himself in a soul-satisfying vocation, to devote himself to some great objective, and to achieve something. There would seem to be nothing against such an hypothesis. On the contrary, if we take seriously the fact that he was man, we must necessarily ascribe to him masculine traits and characteristics.

What then was the position of the Man Jesus with regard to a profession? May it be intelligently asserted that he followed a particular calling? Was this calling of such a nature that it corresponded to his natural dispositions and his spiritual needs? Was it granted him to busy himself with a great achievement or to fulfill himself in following out a great aim?

We accept it more or less as a matter of fact that until his thirteenth year Jesus led a quiet hidden life in Nazareth, and followed the trade of carpenter. When he was about thirty years old he suddenly changed his way of life and entered on that of teacher and preacher. We do not know what natural reasons induced him to forsake carpentry and to adopt the profession of Rabbi, but certain it is that the transition was neither usual nor self-evident. It entailed a decided change of occupation, a total change in his exterior way of life as well as in his immediate goal. The objection does not hold, that in the case of Jesus the interior goal remained always the same: the glory of his heavenly Father, the salvation of souls, the example of a Godly life. That is undoubtedly true. But we do not here speak of the ultimate religious goal, which must remain unchanged in every holy person and in every change of occupation. If, for example, St. Clement Hofbauer * forsook his trade of baker and

---

* *St. Clement Hofbauer, C.SS.R., Patron of Vienna (1751–*

devoted himself to the study of theology, we are not justified in thinking that his ultimate religious focus was changed. Even as a baker he wished to glorify God and to apply himself to the duties of his state in a manner pleasing to God. And yet we speak of a complete change of vocation, and in consideration of the new orientation of his life we speak of him as a "late vocation." His biographers emphasize that as a baker the saint had been restless and discontented, and had suffered much during this long probationary period until God, in His providence, finally removed the obstacles which stood in the way of his true vocation.

May we then consider the life of Jesus from a similar standpoint? Naturally we must reverently refrain from seeing in him a "late vocation" in the merely human sense, but the fact remains that the Will of his heavenly Father held him captive for an unconscionably long time in a calling which can hardly have been congenial or satisfying to his rich natural dispositions or his deep earnest nature. We may confidently assert that the three years of his public life of teaching must have been more gratifying to Jesus than all the long years of his life at the carpenter's bench.

Considered even in its purely external aspect the life of the last three years was incomparably fuller, more versatile and more varied than the hidden life at Nazareth. He was now in the public eye, with unlimited scope for the exercise of all the powers of his glorious manhood. Now he could teach, and preach, console, uplift and heal souls. How his heart must have throbbed with emotion and holy joy as his gaze fell on the multitudes who thronged about him, and with rapt attention hung

1820), by Rev. John Carr, C.SS.R. Published by Sands & Co., London.

on his very words! How willingly and gladly he dispensed to them not only the bread of this earthly life, but much more willingly and much more gladly the bread of eternal life! How overjoyed this man must have been in the innermost recesses of his soul that he could now speak of his heavenly Father, of His Love and His Providence, of His Beauty, and His Immensity, of His Grace and His *Matt.* Generosity. "Out of the abundance of the heart the *xii. 34* mouth speaketh," and we know well what his heart was full of. Now he was enabled to bring forth and dispense his own interior riches; now his manhood could express and fulfill itself in a great work, now he could spend his forces in the pursuit of a sublime aim!

If there ever was a task that could fill and satisfy the life of a holy man it was that in which the man Jesus was now engaged, and we can therefore, fully appreciate the words the evangelist wrote of Jesus when he was at the zenith of his Galilean activity: "In that same hour he *Luke* rejoiced in the Holy Ghost." For he was now in his *x. 21* proper element. Now the great time was come, for which he had had to wait so long.

The perfect conformity to the will of his heavenly Father in which Jesus lived, even in the quietness and hiddenness of his life in Nazareth, does not at all affect his natural inclination of mind and soul, for despite the complete surrender of his Will, in the lower part of his Being he was subject to all the upheavals and contradictions which form part of the heritage of fallen human nature.

This is evidenced for us by his attitude in the Garden of Gethsemane, where, in spite of the most perfect resignation to the will of his Father his whole nature rebelled, even to the sweating of blood, against his ap*Matt.* proaching bodily and mental sufferings. "He began to *xxvi. 37* grow sorrowful and to be sad." And he said: "My soul is sorrowful even unto death. . . . His sweat became as *Luke* drops of blood trickling down upon the ground." *xxii. 44* Theology is unable to explain satisfactorily these phenomena in the spiritual life of Jesus, but the knowledge that they exist should make us cautious in depicting the life of the God-man, and help us to keep in mind that there is in the human nature of Christ, his unity with the Godhead notwithstanding, a whole wide range of natural experiences and emotions the consideration of which need cause us no embarrassment. It simply means that we take seriously the dogma of Faith: "He took flesh, and was made man."

In virtue of such considerations we think it not amiss to suggest that during the years in Nazareth the maturing Man Jesus must have suffered much under the burden of an uncongenial vocation. Could not he have begun his public life at the age of twenty or twenty-five instead of at thirty years of age? Must he not have felt constantly urged to do so by his superior talents, by his profound knowledge of existing contemporary religious and moral exigencies, by his great zeal for the glory of God and by the intensity of his own native energy? But he remained hidden in Nazareth; he stuck to the carpenter's bench. He submitted to the will of his Father in Heaven.

"He advanced in wisdom and age, and grace with *Luke* God and men." How significant must these words appear *ii. 52* to us now? What an excellent testimony to a young man! And from the fact that this divine testimony was made of one who was an ordinary carpenter, we may surmise with what determination, manliness and freedom he lived through those long years of waiting. There is no trace of interior atrophy, or niggardliness, or stultification or bitterness, and in the appointed time he makes his appearance in public, full of balanced energy and courageous enterprise, as if he could not have done so before, and as if he were only now entering into the full maturity of his manhood.

Why then did Jesus thus postpone the moment of his public appearance? Was he held back by the necessity of earning his living? Was he obliged to support his mother? Did the unfavorable social conditions not permit of an earlier release? To all these questions there is no satisfactory answer. Nor is it necessary that we should know the immediate circumstances which governed the decisions of a man who has granted us such a glorious insight into the ultimate reasons which prompted his actions, when he testified of himself: "My meat is to do the will of Him that sent me, that I may perfect His work." Only when the Father called him "were the fields white for the harvest," and only from that time forward did "He that reapeth receive wages, and gather fruit unto life everlasting."

John iv. 34 iv. 36

2. SURE OF HIS VOCATION

In the history of the world there has never been a man whose life, conduct and activity were so completely and unmistakably dominated by the consciousness of a definite mission and divine vocation, as was that of the Man of Nazareth. Other great men there have been who believed they had a mission from which they drew their strength, and because of which they made certain claims to be taken seriously by their fellow-men. But in so far as clarity, certainty and determination are concerned, no comparison is possible between the mission of any other human being and that of Jesus. In this also he was unique. For in the case of all other human beings the conviction that they had a mission to fulfill was arrived at only as a gradual process in the course of their lives, or they gave their activity this interpretation subsequent to certain successes which came their way, or by reason of special fields of action which were opened up to them. But there were periods of depression and uncertainty when they fell a prey to the gravest doubts, when success eluded them, and when contradictions crowded in on them, and when the sense of their responsibility weighed heavy on their souls. At such times they asked themselves in inward horror: "Am I on the right path? Have I undertaken something unworthy? Have I gone too far? Have I been the victim of a delusion? Did God really call me to this work?" History records for us how, on occasion, the souls of the great and mighty ones of this world were tortured and torn by fears and doubts of this nature.

Nothing of all that appears in the life of the Man Jesus. Never once did he betray the slightest trace of uncertainty in the apprehension and interpretation of his life and his work. For him the conviction of a divine mission was not something he arrived at gradually in the course of the years, or a sudden decision taken in the flush of success.

I have designated the years of the quiet, hidden life of Jesus at Nazareth as a time of waiting. That is by no means to suggest that during that time he was in any sense less earnest in the accomplishment of the duties attaching to his state, or that he was as yet unaware of the ultimate purpose of his existence, or that his real vocation was made known to him only gradually and at a later date, perhaps in that powerful religious experience after the baptism in the Jordan. There is no question of anything of that kind.

The life of the Man of Nazareth betrays no inward irresolution, no crises of any kind, nor is there any indication of a gradually awakening consciousness of himself or of his mission. From the very beginning he rejoiced in the peace of a full and perfect certainty. His life and work, even during the uneventful years in Nazareth, unfold themselves as a comprehensive unity in and under a uniquely divine vocation. His first and last recorded words bear strong testimony to this. When his parents were calling the twelve-year-old boy to account for his seemingly thoughtless conduct, he objected: "Did you

Luke ii. 49

not know that I must be in that which is my Father's?" This reply they could have taken as a reference to the temple of stone in which they stood as the house of his heavenly Father. But he meant far more than that. For him the only norm of life was the Will, the Command, the Call of the Father, and so he would give his parents to understand that everything he undertook was to be looked at in the light of obedience to his Father's Will, whether the proximate motives for his acts were apparent or not. And thus he justified his behavior. On the Cross

John xix. 30

he expired with the cry: "It is consummated! Father, into thy hands I commend my spirit." His life as a comprehensive whole, as a mission, as the reason for his coming forth from the Father was consummated. Hence he gave his soul back into the hands of the Father, who had sent and commissioned him.

These two declarations form the framework for the numerous other utterances which help us to judge how clearly and decisively Jesus recognized himself as the one called and sent by God, and how fully and completely he answered that call. It would be necessary to quote whole pages from the Gospels if one were to cite all the passages which prove that Jesus was clearly aware of his mission. It is St. John who attests this most frequently. He sees the Man Jesus really only as he who has come down from above, as he who knew himself to have been sent and called by the Father, and bound by His will. With equal clarity and certainty, Jesus was conscious that his life

must be the fulfillment of all that was written of him in
the Scriptures. Therefore, before he ascended into
Heaven he interpreted and summed-up his life and
work: "These are the words which I spoke to you while *Luke*
I was yet with you, that all things must needs be fulfilled, *xxiv. 44*
which are written in the law of Moses, and in the
prophets, and in the psalms concerning me." Above all
he saw his sufferings as the fulfillment of the prophecies
contained in the Scriptures: "The Son of Man indeed
goeth, as it is written of him." He refused to ask help of *Matt.*
the Father, for "How then shall the scriptures be ful- *xxvi. 24*
filled, that so it must be done." *xxvi. 54*

The life and work of the Man Jesus were in a very
special sense under the direction of the Holy Ghost. With
what reverence and gratitude Jesus must have submitted
himself to this direction, and how earnestly he must have
endeavored to correspond with it in every smallest
detail! "Full of the Holy Ghost" he left the Jordan, and
"was led by the Spirit into the desert." The evangelist *Luke*
Mark uses the strong expression: "the Spirit drove him *iv. 1*
out into the desert." "In the power of the Spirit" he
entered upon his great Galilean mission. He was always
conscious of an interior "time" and "hour" which must
come for the fulfillment of his resolutions. "Your time is
always ready" he said to his relatives who were accus- *John*
tomed to worldly and egoistic ways of thought and *vii. 6*
action. But of himself he avowed: "My time is not yet
come. . . . I go not up to this festival day: because my
time is not accomplished."

Never once was the soul of Jesus overshadowed by the
slightest tinge of doubt or uncertainty as to the meaning
of his mission. He knew himself to be the promised
Messias and the true Son of God, who was to save
the world from sin. That was the mighty mandate
which the Father had given him for his inheritance:

"The son of man is not come to be ministered unto, but
Matt. to minister, and to give his life a redemption for many."
xx. 28 "I came not to call the just but sinners." His task was to
preach and build up the Kingdom of God as he tells us
himself: "To other cities also I must preach the King-
Luke dom of God: for thereto am I sent." It was the King-
iv. 43 dom of God that he taught his Apostles to pray, that
Kingdom which, on the last day, he will give to his own
as their eternal possession.

3. HIS OBEDIENCE TO GOD

The German philosopher, Nietzsche, once proposed to
himself the question, in what true distinction and real
superiority consists. He was of opinion that both postulate
"riches of person." If this subtle assertion be true—and
who will deny it?—the Man Jesus must have personified
unrivalled nobility and superiority, since in him were to
be found the greatest "riches of person," divine riches in
the most literal sense, for as Son of God he was the
second Divine Person, and his divine splendor shed its
luster, its power and its dignity over his human nature.
Therefore, as man also he was Lord and Master. "King
Apoc. of Kings," "Lord of Lords" were the words which St.
xix. 16 John saw written on his garments.

We sometimes meet with people of whom we spontaneously affirm that they are "born gentlemen." On
closer consideration we find that this testimony is exacted
from us by a certain punctiliousness in externals, in
clothing and hearing, in speech, in self-control, and the
maintenance of a certain reserve in dealing with others,
and so on. All that testifies to a certain ideal of nobility
and mastery, to intellectual superiority, to an aristocratic
character in the best sense of the word.

Shall we, when we speak of the superiority of the Man
Jesus, conjure up a similar picture? Yes and no! Cer-

tainly not, in the sense that we must dissociate him from anything artificial, acquired, superimposed or insincere. His superiority and mastery were truer, deeper, richer, more obviously innate. In him everything pointed to a nobility unique, unrivalled and incomparable, a superiority which completely overshadowed anything merely human.

In what does the secret of true superiority consist? Not in the lordship over lands, nor even in dominion over the wills of others. Real superiority is a quality inherent in the human being which expresses itself as firmness, consciousness of dignity, the sense of power and self-reliance, the urge to create and the joy of effort. Such superiority, however, does not postulate independence of a higher will. It must not be confused with autocracy. The essential thing is that the bond with the higher will legitimately exists, is clearly recognized and given interior acquiescence. The subordinate then participates in the dignity and worth of the over-lord, and reflects his superiority.

Thus it is that we understand the superiority of Christ which unfolds itself as a participation in the absolute sovereignty of the Father. For he did not merely acknowledge his subordination to the will of his heavenly Father; he acquiesced in it with his whole strength and embraced it with the full force of his human freedom. "I do not my own will" he tells us, "but the will of Him that sent me." And he interprets the doing of his Father's *John* will as his "meat"; the fulfilling of God's work as his all- *v. 30* sufficing task in life. He did not doubt or mistrust in any way this subordination to the sovereign will of God, nor did he harbor any fear for the consequent freedom or independence of his own person. On the contrary, he regarded this unconditional surrender to the will of the Father, the obedience to God as the purest and most glorious completion of his superiority. St. Paul reveals a deep appreciation of the superiority of the Man Jesus when he tells us that he became "obedient unto death, even to the death of the Cross. For which cause God also hath exalted him, and hath given him a name which is above all names: that in the name of Jesus every knee should bow . . ., and that every tongue should confess that the Lord Jesus Christ is in the glory of God the Father."

Phil. viii. 11.

The incomparable superiority of Jesus, therefore, rested on the solid foundations of religious conviction, and his healthy, virile piety. Religion for Jesus meant the union of the whole man with God, of the intellect with the truth of God, of the will with the commandments of God. His self-reliance reflected the calm and imperturbability of the Almighty. "Government is upon his shoulders," says the prophet Isaias, not as an oppressive burden, but as a participation in the omnipotence and authority of God, as "the fullness of the glory of God."

Isaias ix. 5

How different is such superiority from that gospel which is promulgated in modern times, the doctrine of autonomy, the self-glorification of man! "Man is his own master." So runs the gospel of the new superiority. A new faith and a new religion are preached, not a faith in the one, true, transcendent God, as Christianity teaches, not religion as the union of man with the revealed truth, and his subordination to the laws of his Creator. Such a conception of truth and religion is regarded as old-fashioned and altogether unworthy of modern, emancipated man, who acknowledges, to be sure, his subjection to certain primitive laws of being and life, but will not acknowledge any obligations or restrictions from above, from a personally conceived God. The Ten Commandments, he is told, rob man of his rightful freedom and independence. They must be adapted and modernized. It is they that destroy man's superiority.

Let us for a moment consider this attitude. Does the modern doctrine of autonomy give man real freedom, stability and security? Is it, in Christ's words, a good tree giving forth good fruit?

A religion which binds man from below rather than from above and upwards towards a personal God is, in fact, not a religion except in name. Nobody but a fool will dream of denying that man is bound by the laws of nature and of life and in many ways dependent on them. But the recognition of such bonds does not by any means constitute a religious man, and such a comparison falsifies the very notion of religion and robs it of its content. Does not the uniqueness, the incomparability, the holiness of real religion consist in that man finds himself bound to the invisible, transcendent God? The consciousness of such union man may deny, perhaps even supplant, but never abolish or altogether uproot from his heart.

If man is conscious of no upward obligation towards God, if he recognizes not the will of God over him, then he sets himself up as the supreme being; he makes himself a God. And then we have a paradoxical situation. For on the one hand, man, by reason of his intellect and freedom, stands superior to nature, whose laws he may sporadically evade, or by artificial interference cause to deviate, or even temporarily eliminate, while, on the other hand, he finds himself drifting helplessly before their superior force. A weakling God. Truly a laughable figure, a very caricature of superiority!

Modern man will take for his guide the whisperings of his own soul. Yes, if only such whisperings were always unmistakably clear and perceptible! If only one had always the assurance that they were directed towards the right and the good! But many whisperings and rustlings there are in our souls, good and evil, true and false, angelic voices and diabolical mutterings. Only a fool would attempt to deny this fact. Does not the criminal also appeal to the voice of nature and follow his natural tendencies? And who can hold it against him that he misinterprets them, if there are no binding commandments of God for his guidance?

For the commandments of God contain the interpretation of the real, true laws of life, and from them we may read what corresponds to our nature. They indicate for us the path of true liberty and success, and have nothing in them that is antiquated, superfluous, or repulsive to nature.

The genuine superiority which the soul of man craves consists then not only in obligations from below from the depths of our nature and the constraint of our natural impulses, but also, and far more essentially, in obligations upward to our Lord and God, the Creator of mankind. Such obligations are not in any way a humiliating restriction or violation of man's freedom; on the contrary, they help him to keep his house in order, and save him from the slavery of error and the chaotic confusion of a life ruled by blind impulse.

Matt. vii. 20 "By their fruits ye shall know them." The fruits of the arrogant, self-glorification of modern man are already quite apparent. There is first the anxiety and uncertainty which torture the soul of the man who refuses to acknowledge the existence of a loving, omnipotent, omniscient God, and who feels himself tossed as flotsam and jetsam on the waves of blind chance, whose vaunted authority is but a mockery, and for whom nothing remains but a gloomy abandonment to fate. In vain does he seek to stamp his attitude as superiority; it is, in reality, nothing more than an all-too-obvious attempt to cloak his fundamental confusion and embarrassment.

The second bitter fruit which autonomous man must taste is that of isolation and loneliness. And where is he to turn in his deep, intolerable loneliness if there is no personal God with whom he may share his thoughts and aspirations? The voices of nature and the powers of the deep have no answer to his tortured pleadings. He stands abysmally alone. By superficiality, or by plunging himself into the hustle and bustle of life, he may, perhaps, in some measure temporarily lull himself into the false equanimity of those who refuse to think, but such an attitude is infinitely removed from the quiet, true, dignified liberating and invulnerable superiority which is the product of obedience to God, and a participation in His own sovereign authority.

The life of the Man of Nazareth gloriously illustrates and reflects this sublime nobility, superiority and authority.

4. TRUE TO HIS MISSION

Jesus was the Messias and the Son of God who came into the world to redeem mankind, and it was as such that he was to manifest himself. That was the Father's command. At first, however, his message was not intended for mankind in general, but for his own people, the Jews of that age, for he "was not sent but to the sheep that are lost of the house of Israel." *Matt. xv. 24*

The duty of self-revelation signified in itself a heavy and painful task for the Man Jesus. Having become like us in all things, he lived as a man among men, and now he was to come forward with the claim that he was really and truly God. What unheard-of presumption! And what an exacting demand on the critical minds of his hearers! It was a claim that might have won a measure of credence among the pagans of the Hellenistic world, who were somewhat familiar with the idea that one of their many deities might at any time make his appearance on the earth in human form; and there were many legends extant of such "incarnations" and visible appearances of the pagan divinities amongst the men of old. But even here his claim would have met with the most violent antagonism, for he was not merely a god among gods, but the only-begotten Son of the One, true, all-holy God of whom the pagans knew nothing.

But the divine command sent him not to the pagans but to the Jews. And for them his appearance signified the great hour of the national re-awakening.

There were three treasured national possessions which the Israelites had claimed for centuries as peculiarly their own: the belief in the one true God; the expectation of the coming Messias and Redeemer of mankind; and the law given to them by God in the Covenant on Mount Sinai with its glorious system of worship.

"They are Israelites, to whom belongeth the adoption as of children, and the glory, and the testament, and the giving of the law, and the service of God, and the *Rom.* promises." Thus does St. Paul in his Epistle to the *ix. 4* Romans pay tribute to the spiritual and religious wealth of his people. But that which was bestowed on them by God to be to them a "pedagogue unto Christ" became rather a colossal impediment to their acceptance of Christ when he made his appearance among them.

The belief in one only God as contrasted with the polytheism of the heathen constituted the great pride of the Israelites. But in the course of the centuries they had concentrated so exclusively on the Unity of the Godhead that any notion of plurality in the divine Being itself must have seemed to them unthinkable, intolerable, even blasphemous. And so they placed their humanly-conceived idea of God above his new self-revelation. How could any mere man, even though he moved in the plane of the all-holy and claimed for himself divine attributes, count on being heard by such people? Yet the plain, simple Man Jesus, the insignificant carpenter of Nazareth, the son of Joseph, must now come before them with precisely this claim! To be sure he worked great miracles which testified to the truth of his claim, he went very circumspectly to work in order to avoid giving unnecessary offence, he was very restrained in his utterances and carefully avoided any direct reference to himself as God or the Son of God; he even forbade the demons, whom he had expelled, to give him this title, lest there should be any misunderstanding. But despite his prudence the theologians and intellectual leaders among the people soon noticed what he was aiming at. It was inevitable that they should do so, for he was compelled to reveal himself, he dared not disavow himself and his true nature and suppress the message of the heavenly Father.

Were the Jews guiltless in their disbelief? This question is not our primary consideration here. Christ himself answered it when he said: "If I had not come, and spoken to them, they would not have sin: but now they have no excuse for their sin." Our chief concern is to show how extremely difficult it must have been for the Man Jesus "to speak to them," to present himself before these people with his sublime, supernatural claim, how he had to condone and at the same time condemn their behavior when they stooped down to pick up stones to throw at the supposed blasphemer, and how little surprised, and yet how deeply hurt, he must have been when he heard their questions: "Is not this Jesus the son of Joseph, whose father and mother we know? How then saith he, I came down from heaven? Who art thou? Whom dost thou make thyself?" In a short time tension had reached such a pitch that every unequivocal self-

John
xv. 22

John
xv. 22

John
vi. 42

confession on his part was fraught with danger to his life. But the Man Jesus took refuge neither in silence, nor evasion. He remained true to his mission.

Jesus was the promised Messias who had been expected by the Jews. All the hopes of the Jewish nation were centered around the figure of the Messias. Of him the prophets spoke. In times of difficulty and national stress the people took comfort in the thought of the great and powerful leader who was to come and who would lead them to victory. The most daring comparisons, the most enticing promises, the most shattering threats colored their words when they spoke of him, rousing the people to thought and action, and awakening in them new hope and fresh courage. In the person of the Messias everything stood or fell. And now in the Man of Nazareth he appeared in the flesh.

Luke xviii. 8

"But yet the son of man when he cometh, shall he find, think you, faith on earth?" In formulating this question Jesus would give expression to his own painful experience that not all men brought to the Messias an open mind and a believing heart. Only they who were genuinely holy found the interior way to him. It was quite otherwise with the Scribes and Pharisees and the leaders of the people. *They* knew the Scriptures. *They* knew exactly what was written therein concerning the Messias. But they had painted over and defaced the Scriptural portrait of the Messias with the brush of their self-love and national greed for power. The Messias, whom they would welcome, must establish an earthly kingdom, lead the Jews to political supremacy, and ensure for them a life of wealth, sensuality and eternal youth. Thus they interpreted the sayings of the prophets in many of their religious tracts which they circulated along with the Scriptures.

This portrait of the Messias was a direct contradiction

of all that the true Messias preached and practiced. And it was not merely that the word "Messias" carried a firmly-established interpretation; but the mere use of the word was taken as an acknowledgment that one accepted this interpretation and placed one, so to speak, on the side of the Scribes and Pharisees. Hence it obviously was a highly difficult and delicate task for the Man Jesus to proclaim himself the Messias, for if in the mere use of the word there was danger of being misunderstood, how much more unthinkable it was that he should identify his person with the notion of the Messias current in authoritative circles. In actual fact we notice that as far as possible he avoided applying to himself the title Messias and used instead the equally messianic, but less compromising term "Son of Man." But even this gave offense. Many of those who in the early stages had believed in him because of the miracles he worked, felt disappointed in him. He had not fulfilled their political expectations. Nationalistic fanatics and adventurers in underground movements, who were only waiting for a favorable opportunity to take arms against the hated Romans, tried to win him over to their side, thus jeopardizing his whole work. Finally the Pharisees could contain themselves no longer, and, misinterpreting his reticence, they reproached him bitterly: "How long dost thou hold our souls in suspense? If thou be the Christ tell us plainly." *John x. 24ff.* And how truthfully could Jesus reply: "I speak to you, and you believe not: the works that I do in the name of my Father, they give testimony of me. But you do not believe."

To what a tragic pass the Jewish leaders had been brought by their obstinacy. All their hopes, religious and national, had been based on the person of the promised Messias. And now that he stood before them in the flesh, they were so blinded by their pride and selfishness that they could not recognize him.

Equally tragic was the fate of the Man Jesus. With what burning desire he wished to manifest himself to his unhappy people as the Messias and Redeemer! Yet now that he stood before them he hardly dared to say that he was the Son of Man lest he should be taken for someone quite other than he was. And still the command of the Father lay heavy on him.

The third religious and national possession of the Jews was the law. None of the pagan peoples boasted such a superior moral code or such a highly organized system of regulations as was laid down in the sacred writings of the Jews. Of that the Israelites might well be proud. And in actual fact the Scribes and Pharisees were inordinately proud of it, so proud that they literally worshipped the law. The letter superseded the spirit, the knowledge of the law the practice of it, the form took preference over the content: "They bind heavy, and unsupportable burdens: and lay them on men's shoulders: but with a *Matt.* finger of their own they will not move them." In these *xxiii. 4ff.* scathing words Jesus once described the behavior of the Scribes and Pharisees, which drew from his lips the terrible condemnation contained in the twenty-third chapter of St. Matthew's Gospel: "Woe to you Scribes and Pharisees, hypocrites: because you tithe mint, and anise, and cummin, and have left the weightier things of the law, judgement, and mercy, and faith . . . you *Matt.* make clean the outside of the cup and of the dish: but *xxiii. 23ff.* within you are full of rapine and uncleanness."

To these hypocritical devotees of the letter of the law Jesus had to announce the new law of the interior spirit, love and purity. To them he had to say: The descent from Moses avails you nothing, the external observance of the law avails you nothing if you are not converted

interiorly! And before them he had to confess: The Son
of Man is greater than Solomon, greater than John,
greater than Abraham, Lord of the Temple, Lord of the
Sabbath! He, the humble and insignificant Rabbi, the
simple Man from Nazareth! What patience, prudence,
control and consideration were necessary for such a task!

What misunderstanding, hostility, hatred, threats and
persecution he would have to submit to! But he pursued
his task bravely and indefatigably. There was no trace of
uncertainty or uneasiness, fear or timidity in him; neither
was there anything of that blind fanaticism, born perhaps
of concealed anxiety. He was always and everywhere
perfectly self-possessed, always master of the situation,
always abreast of the claims made on him. He neither
concealed nor suppressed anything. He spoke boldly and
openly as the occasion required, even at the risk of his
life. Occasionally we find him complaining to his friends
of the disbelief which he encountered but his complaint
is tempered with mildness, his wrath breathes holiness.
All objections against his claims and demands came to
nothing. He always had right on his side; he was what
he claimed to be. Nobody could complain at any time
that the truth was too harshly flung in his face, and so
in the supper-room before his Passion he was able to
confess to his Father in absolute sincerity of heart:
"Father, I have finished the work which thou gavest me
to do. . . . I have manifested thy name to the men
whom thou hast given me out of the world. . . . Now
they have known that all things which thou hast given
me are from thee: Because the words which thou gavest
me, I have given to them: and they have received them
and have known in very deed that I came out from thee, *John*
and they have believed that thou didst send me." *xvii. 4ff.*

To be sure, the little band of believers was at first very
small; the Apostles and some few men besides, and a

number of pious women from Jerusalem and Galilee who had attached themselves to him were all he could count as his followers. But the chief aim of the Man Jesus was not the immediate success of his work, but rather the loyal and unflinching effort to accomplish the task which the Father had laid upon him.

In this role of ambassador of the heavenly Father the Apocalypse bears him the most glorious testimony: he was "the faithful witness."

5. MIGHTY IN WORD AND DEED

When the two disciples were relating to the stranger who had joined them on their way to Emmaus their experiences while in the company of Jesus of Nazareth, they summed up their impressions of him in the words: *Luke xxiv. 19* "He was a prophet, mighty in work and word before all the people."

Jesus was a man in the mysterious fullness of power and strength which shone forth in his life and work. He had the gift of miracles. The reality and boundlessness of this gift, coupled with the sovereignty with which he availed himself of it, and the sanctity with which he invested it most strikingly emphasize the beauty of his manhood. And it was this impression that won from the lips of the two disciples the words of praise quoted above.

History has preserved for us the names of great and mighty men who accomplished heroic deeds, astonished the world, and enkindled in the breasts of men burning fires of enthusiasm. But all the admiration notwithstanding, it nevertheless remained obvious that their power and capacity were confined within well-defined limits, and it was undreamt of that they should overstep the boundaries of the natural and possible. With the Man Jesus it was quite otherwise; *his* power seemed to transcend all human limitations.

It was the proximity and efficacy of this power that won him general admiration. Jesus made no mere speeches about how a great and mighty man should look and indulged in no phantasies about the effect of unlimited power, for the Man Jesus *possessed* the power; daily and hourly he availed himself of this great gift as lightly and spontaneously as of the gestures of his hands and the cadences of his voice. In his presence one was standing before unlimited greatness, power and possibility and refrained from seeking further. People gazed, and wondered, and then burst forth in admiration; they praised God "Who had given such power to men." *Matt. ix. 8*

His power extended to all the different spheres of being. All nature obeyed him; the turbulent waters of the lake, the fish that lived therein, the fig-tree, the loaves and fishes. He healed all manner of disease and infirmity: the leprous, the fever-stricken, the lame, the blind, the deaf, the dumb, the woman with the issue of blood, the man with the withered hand, the dropsical man, the mentally deranged and the infirm woman. He saw into the hearts of men and read their thoughts and intentions. St. John the Evangelist says of him: "He knew all men, and needed not that any should give testimony of man: for he knew what was in man." His *John ii. 25* vision embraced the future. Thus he described in detail the sufferings of his coming Passion, he knew in advance of the treachery of Judas, of the denial of Peter, of the exaltation of Mary of Bethany, the stability of the Church and the strengthening work of the Holy Ghost. He manifested his supremacy over the evil spirits who left their victims and fled at his word or at his mere approach. And the angels of God came and ministered to him. Death itself acknowledged his dominion, and a consideration of the three miracles of raising the dead to life reveals a certain upward progression in the manifestation of his power. First he restored to life the daughter of Jairus who had only just died, then the widow's son who was being taken out for burial, and finally the man Lazarus who had been for some days in the grave. How majestically authoritative his commands sound: "Maiden, I say to thee, arise." "Young man, I say to thee, arise." "Lazarus, come forth."

He possessed extraordinary sway over the hearts of men. His person radiated a mysterious attraction. A word from him sufficed to command obedience. He governed the will of others. One day on his way to Galilee he met a man. Jesus looked at him and said: *John i. 43* "Follow me." Philip followed him and became an Apostle. Passing by, he saw Levi the son of Alpheus sitting in the custom-house. To him likewise he addressed the call: "Follow me." Levi immediately responded, abandoned his lucrative profession and attached himself to Jesus. Near the Sea of Galilee he met the brothers, Peter and Andrew, who were about to go fishing. "Come *Mark i. 16–20* after me," he said to them, "and I will make you to become fishers of men." And immediately they left their nets and followed him. By the exercise of the same power he saved himself from the violence of his enemies, for we read that, when the inhabitants of Nazareth would have thrown him over a cliff, "he passing through the *Luke iv. 30* midst of them, went his way." And in the Garden of Gethsemane the soldiers were able to bind him only when he permitted it. Thus he verified in all his dealings with men the truth of the words he spoke to the governor Pontius Pilate: "Thou shouldst not have any power *John xix. 11* against me, unless it were given thee from above," for he was himself the source of the power, which others used against him.

Jesus worked his miracles in an infinite variety of ways. The most ceremonious, if one may use the word, of all

his miracles were the healing of the blind man of Bethsaida and the cure of the man born blind. And lest the
manner of working these miracles should lead to the
erroneous conclusion that Jesus could use his power only
in a certain predetermined way, there are others in plenty
to prove that he was absolutely free and independent of
exterior circumstances. He healed the Centurion's servant from a distance by a mere assurance, and in like
manner the daughter of the Canaanite woman. Many
were healed by the mere touch of his hand, as, for
instance, Peter's mother-in-law; others by a word of
command, as the lame man; while on other occasions
miracles were worked almost unobtrusively under his
hands or in his presence, as the changing of water into
wine, or the miraculous draught of fishes and the multiplication of the loaves. Often it sufficed for the sick
person to touch the hem of his garment or the tassel of
his cloak in order to be healed.

The main source of the power of the Man Jesus lay in
the unity of his human nature with the second Divine
Person, and so it was becoming that his human nature
should be distinguished by all the graces and mystical
gifts of which a created being is capable. The living
temple of God had to be endowed with a splendor in
keeping with its dignity. And the unlimited power of
miracles belonged to the mystical gifts and could not be
separated from the mystery of his Person. He was no
juggler or magician who displayed the tricks of his trade
before a public greedy for sensation, and then withdrew
into his insignificant private life. The main point was
always himself, his Person, with whom this power was
inseparably united, the sovereign Lord, at whose disposal
he held this power which he did not use to create a sensation, whether he uncovered the secret thoughts of
others or called the dead from their graves, whether he

stilled the hunger of the crowd with a few loaves, or commanded the wind and the waves to be calm.

Always and everywhere he was the perfect master of himself, and his power revealed itself as a perfectly controlled force and in accordance with certain well-defined principles.

The power which a man has may easily become for him a temptation. For he may easily be caught up into the ecstasy of power, the illusion of greatness and the passion to rule. Then the man is no longer the master but the slave of his own power. He loses control of himself. Pride and caprice make him their plaything, and lead him on to the abuse of his power. He becomes a tyrant, an exploiter, an oppressor.

How different in the case of Jesus! Astonishing and unlimited though his power was, it yet remained utterly within his control. He was master of it. He exercised it on occasions when we might not have expected it, and refrained from the use of it on other occasions when an exhibition of power would seem to be called for. But he never, for a single instant, ceased to be master of himself. One will search the Gospels in vain for an instance of where he lost self-control or indulged in misuse of his power. There is never a trace of caprice or frivolity or irritation or uncontrolled behavior even when the crowds pressed him hardest. For his was a thoroughly holy power, and he used it with a sense of the highest moral responsibility. His miracles awakened in those who witnessed them a sense of the special nearness of God. They disposed people to holiness. The wonder-worker edified by his extraordinary deeds, for people saw God at work, and their astonishment frequently found expression in the praise of God. Sinners repented and were converted. In this connection the reaction of Peter to the miraculous draught of fishes is worthy of note. On witnessing the miracle, he fell on his knees before Jesus and said: "Depart from me, for I am a sinful man, O Lord."

Luke v. 8

In accordance with what principles did Jesus use the unlimited power that was his? Any exercise of his thaumaturgical powers was intimately related to his role of prophet and redeemer, provoked by his unparalleled holiness, and had God for its goal. Not once did he use his miraculous gift to subserve or supplement his natural abilities. He travelled on foot, he ate and drank, sent his Apostles to buy food, crossed the lake in a boat, in short, he lived and acted just as other men. Nor did he ever work a miracle merely to overcome natural infirmities, illnesses or deficiencies. And to suppose that by reason of excess of sympathy or softness of heart he was unable to tolerate illness or suffering in his vicinity would be to draw an utterly false picture of him. If that were so he would have healed all those who came his way without exception. But it was not so. At the Pool of Bethsaida there lay "a great multitude of sick, of blind, of lame, of withered, waiting for the moving of the water." Jesus healed only one of them, a man who had been ill for 38 years.

John v. 1ff.

For him it was not a question of doing all that he could do. His criterion was not the law of might, but the principles of holiness and morality. His thaumaturgy never provided him merely with an opportunity for idle, frivolous experiment of his miraculous powers or as a means of satisfying the curiosity and thirst for sensation in others. There was no vulgar display of power, such as he has been accredited with in the spurious Gospels. For this reason he rejected the suggestions of the tempter that he should work a miracle: "It is written: Thou shalt not tempt the Lord thy God." And he refused to work a miracle where faith or good intentions were lacking, as was the case in his home-

Matt. iv. 1ff.

town Nazareth. Mark's account of his attitude there runs: "He could not do any miracles there, only that he cured a few that were sick, laying his hands upon them.
Mark vi. 5 And he wondered because of their unbelief." Above all the thaumaturgical powers of Jesus had nothing of the occult in them. He was neither medium nor hypnotist and the faith which he often demanded as a prerequisite to a miracle was not mere suggestion but a purely religious sentiment.

But Jesus used his miraculous powers primarily to
John xi. 42 prove his divine mission, "that they may believe that thou hast sent me." This proof he owed to his people, if he would have them believe in his divine and messianic person, and without this power his self-revelation would have been impracticable and inconceivable. With it, however, he was able to substantiate and verify his reference to himself. "Though you will not believe me,
John x. 38 v. 36 believe my works." "The works themselves, which I do, give testimony of me." This was the reason why he occasionally worked a miracle with full solemnity and in the presence of certain picked witnesses, as the curing of the lame man in Capharnaum. The Scribes and Pharisees who were present on that occasion were offended because he said to the sick man: "Son, thy sins are for-
Mark ii. 1ff. given thee," and they thought within themselves: "Why doth this man speak thus?" he blasphemeth. Who can forgive sins, but God only?" Jesus read their thoughts and said to them: "Why think you these things in your hearts? Which is easier, to say to the sick of the palsy: Thy sins are forgiven thee; or to say: Arise, take up thy bed and walk? But that you may know that the son of man hath power on earth to forgive sins he saith to the sick of the palsy: I say to thee, arise, take up thy bed, and go into thy house."

He used his power to substantiate startling prophecies,

as, for instance, at the cursing of the fig-tree, or to give warning of future events, as when he himself interpreted the miraculous draught of fishes for Peter in the words: "Fear not: from henceforth thou shalt catch men." He considered it a necessary part of their spiritual formation and apostolic schooling that they should on occasion be witnesses to his miracles, as they were at the Transfiguration and the multiplication of the loaves, and the calming of the storm. By miracles such as the casting out of devils he testified to the coming redemption and the imminent liberation of burdened humanity. He indicated the miracles he had worked as a reply to the Baptist's question: "Art thou he that art to come?" But many of his miracles were prompted solely by his divine goodness and generosity and by his love for tortured humanity.

Luke v. 10

Matt. xi. 2ff.

In the use of his miraculous powers Jesus stands before us a great and mighty man. With majestic self-assurance he meets all dangers, difficulties and suspicion. But his miracles were but the revelation of his essence, and he himself is always the great, incomprehensible miracle, as in the fullness of his power he reveals as man the infinite power and goodness of God.

6. FOUNDER OF THE KINGDOM OF GOD

When one considers the many references made by Jesus to the kingdom of God in his teaching and preaching, the many parables he delivered in order to make clear its origin, nature and value, and how much it obviously meant to him that his Apostles and others should accept and take to heart this notion of the kingdom of God one cannot but conclude that he regarded the founding and propagation of this kingdom, and the establishment of the dominion of God on earth as his divinely ordained task here below. His heart was centered in that work. To it he devoted all his virile powers and strength, and so well did he accomplish it that towards the end of his life he was able to confess to his heavenly Father: "I have finished the work which thou gavest me to do." The message of God's kingdom comprises the whole of Christ's teaching, and to the question: "What has the Man Jesus achieved in his life?" may be given the all-sufficient answer: He was the founder of the kingdom of God.

John xvii. 4

But Jesus of Nazareth was not the first to speak of this kingdom. John the Baptist had done so before him, and even he was not the originator of the idea. Both Jesus and John the Baptist spoke of the kingdom of God as of something already familiar to their audiences, and both opened their mission with the shattering cry: "Do penance, for the kingdom of God is at hand." But though the notion was already inherent in the traditional religious possession of the Jewish people, Jesus could not adopt it ready-made, as it were. For his interpretation of the kingdom of God was not to be found in the Old Testament, or in contemporary rabbinical and apocalyptic writings. They merely offered him possible starting points.

The whole tradition of the kingdom of God runs through the history of Israel in two channels, whose waters mingle occasionally without ever uniting clearly and permanently in one single stream. The one channel is the idea of the kingship of God. Jahve is Lord and King of the whole world, and at the end of time He will finally vindicate his authority by a strict judgment of all his subjects. The second branch of tradition favors the idea of a redeemer-king. From the house of David there will arise a royal scion, who, at the end of time, after the annihilation of all God's enemies, will establish a new era, and a new paradisial kingdom of Justice and Peace. In what relationship the scion of David will stand to God, whether he will establish the sovereignty of God on earth, whether God will direct the world and assert His dominion through him—all that was hinted at but never clearly expressed. Only the prophet Daniel combines the two streams of tradition. According to him the "Son of Man" appears in the clouds of Heaven, that is in his divine capacity, and God will bestow on him "dominion, honour and kingdom." Parallel with this *Dan.* purely religious temporal hope, for the fulfillment of *vii. 13ff.* which the pious Jew prayed daily, there existed a second temporal expectation of a national and political nature in which God was envisaged primarily as the God of Israel. At the end of time God will again restore the kingdom of the Israelite people with the Messias as King thereof, giving it a brilliance and splendor never before possessed by it, and subjugating all other peoples to it. These temporal expectations, religious and national, were cherished by pious Jewish folk, and their expansion catered for by a rich religious literature, but they were never brought into close relationship with one another, and nowhere is it found expressed that the Kingdom of the Messias is the visible assertion of the Divine dominion or that the Messias by his activity would establish the Kingship of God.

We can now appreciate how straight and hard Jesus aimed and hit at the religious and political circles among his people when he placed his collective activity under the motto of the kingdom of God, and began his mission with the call to penance. From all sides and all camps his words must have been echoed back to him. The great discussion about his person was initiated. He had challenged it. That was a manly, creative act of the highest order.

In his conception and teaching of the kingdom of

God, Jesus embraced all the positive, existing elements in the rich, religious tradition of his people into one great, unified and sharply-outlined form. He combined and completed the scattered references from the Old Testament. He purified the apocalyptic writings of their grotesque descriptions and legendary overgrowths and restored them to their purely religious character. Only a clear, ordered, creative spirit such as his could have attempted this gigantic task. For him it was not a question of a mere theory or abstract theology of the kingdom of God, but the realization of the plan of redemption, of the work of the self-revelation and self-communication of God to mankind, of the creative renewal of the world, of the restoration of Israel in a much wider and more glorious sense than that conceived and understood by prophets and Apostles and the pious among the people. A man was here active as master in a building whose grandeur and sublimity will be an ever-lasting testimony to the breadth and the depth, to the versatility and splendor of his spirit.

With what joy, with what creative desire must he have labored at his sublime task. He knew himself to be king in his Kingdom, yea, he was himself the kingdom, the kingship of God in person. In him, and with him, it made its appearance in the world, it was revealed to souls of goodwill and humility as the mighty, hitherto unrevealed mystery exacting from all final, unconditional acquiescence. He knew himself as the Son of Man who would one day come in the clouds of heaven and at the Father's command judge all the peoples of the earth.

The kingdom, which he founded, was his Father's kingdom. Its purpose was the glorification of the Father, and the establishment of His dominion on earth. For this goal the heart of Jesus was aflame with zeal; for this he wished to live and die; in this he saw the realization of his life's task.

But the kingdom of God was also his own, the kingdom for which he taught us to pray daily, which from the foundation of the world has been prepared for the blessed of his Father. The Father had bequeathed it to him as the reward for his personal exertions, the glorious fruit of his manly efforts. Hence he likewise as king was able to promise to his Apostles that they would eat and drink at *his* table in *his* kingdom, and sit upon thrones judging the twelve tribes of Israel. Hence also the assured answer to the governor, Pilate: "My Kingdom is not of this world." *Luke xxii. 30 John xviii. 36*

Let us ponder for a moment the monumental proportions of this divine edifice as testimony to the glorious creative strength of its founder, this living temple which far more than the material Temple of Jerusalem calls forth the cry of astonishment: "Behold . . . what buildings are here." For the foundations of this temple rest in the depths of the Godhead. Its walls withstand even the assaults of hell. Its proportions embrace the whole world. Its arches span time and eternity. *Matt. xiii. 1*

The work of Jesus was intended not only for the nation which gave him birth. He established no mere human society. He founded no school of philosophy. He thought of the men of all times and of all nations, all were meant to find themselves redeemed, at home and safe within the frontiers of his kingdom: learned theologians and plain, simple men, the poor in spirit, the mourners, the meek, the merciful, the persecuted and rejected, canonized saints and struggling sinners: "theirs is the kingdom of Heaven."

But in spite of the burning ardor of his heart Jesus was a clear thinker. His kingdom was not, indeed, of this world, but it must propagate itself in this world, embrace the men of this world and hold its own in the struggle against the powers of this world. Therefore, he would give it a visible form and social anchorage, thus making it correspond to his own Being, to which belongs the visible human nature just as truly as the divine, and to the peculiarity of its members who are composed of a visible body and an invisible soul. He established his kingdom as a visible Church. Quietly and unostentatiously the work of foundation was carried out, so quietly that the first members were utterly unaware of the stupendous work being effected in and through them.

The Church of Christ was at first intended for the Jewish people, and it was to the Israelites exclusively that Jesus directed his first proclamation of the kingdom of God. He was conscious of having been sent by his Father "to the lost sheep of the house of Israel." To it referred the prophetic promises. To be sure, only on condition that they would become converted and prove themselves loyal to the principles of the new kingdom. It presupposed a complete conversion from their pharisaical self-righteousness, from their idolatrous worship of the letter of the law, from their national narrow-mindedness and arrogant contempt of the heathen. Israel according to the flesh would have to become converted to the Israel of the spirit. To the heathen too, the gate of the kingdom of Heaven should be wide open.

But Jesus soon made the bitter discovery that the first chosen would not throw open the door even of their own hearts to his message. The ruling class among his people remained obdurate. Yet Jesus did not give way to despair. With quiet, vigorous, virile determination he called his Apostles, twelve men from among all classes of the people, men of unprejudiced mind and real piety, but, humanly speaking, otherwise quite unqualified to act as pioneers of God's kingdom and pillars of the universal

Church. These men he set about training for the mighty task he had in view for them, and this activity of his will repay consideration, since it affords us a valuable insight into the manner in which by means of hard, unremitting work, and in the face of bitter disappointment, he founded his Kingdom in the hearts of his hearers. For Jesus was no unpractical, dreamy idealist who preached sublime doctrines but remained aloof and detached from the hard realities of life. In the kingdom of his Father he had risen from the ranks. He has left no writings to posterity. He rejected everything in the nature of propaganda for his person or his work. He never left the confines of Palestine. He made no special studies, sought out none of the noted cultural centers of the day. None sought success, or thirsted for the adulation of men so little as he. Yet no other historical personality ever radiated such a powerful and enduring influence, on the thought and actions and moral outlook of men as did Jesus Christ. His whole work was nothing but a reflection of his Being, edification in the best and fullest sense of the word.

Jesus had taught, preached, worked many miracles and experienced phenomenal success. He had been acclaimed, admired, lionized by the people. Yet what remained to him ultimately of all this? Did it grow and become world-success? By no means! The multitudes who had acclaimed him in Galilee, who at his entrance into the Holy City had spread their garments on the streets before him to do homage to the Son of David, shouted on Good Friday: "Away with him. Crucify him. We have no other king but Caesar." At the foot of his Cross only a handful of loyal souls summoned up courage to confess themselves his followers. And at his death St. Luke gives the number of his followers as about one hundred and twenty! The fact is that of the fruits of his

John xix. 15

own personal activity scarcely a vestige remained. Only in very few loyal hearts did the message of Jesus work straightforwardly and uninterruptedly: in the Apostles, and even in them not without a sharp crisis during the days of the Passion, in the pious women who had followed him from Galilee, and in a few unnamed disciples. That was the ultimate tangible fruit of the preaching of Jesus. He did not aim at mass conversions, but tried by the power of his personality to win individual souls to his kingdom. "The kingdom of Heaven is like to leaven, *Matt.* which a woman took and hid in three measures of *xiii. 33* meal, until the whole was leavened." In this little parable we are given the secret of his method. By his mere existence, by his whole character, by the formative influence of his personal example he worked as a leaven in his surroundings: quietly, effectively, inconspicuously and yet with tremendous power.

And so he won his Apostles for the kingdom of God. His radiant personality convinced them more than his individual teachings, more even than his miracles. They sensed the mystery of his Godhead and believed in him. And he endowed them with the necessary authority, and at the end of his life gave them the world-wide mission: "Going therefore, teach ye all nations, baptising them in the name of the Father, and of the Son, and of the Holy Ghost . . . and behold I am with you all days even to *Matt.* the consummation of the world."
xxviii. 19

In his Church the Man Jesus effected a unique work. It has no parallel, either in the manner of its foundations, or in its internal and external structure, or in its supernal goal. With the minimum of means he achieved the maximum result. Consider the mean, almost contemptible beginning from which this universal, twenty-century old kingdom took its rise! At the very outset his dearly-won little congregation threatened to collapse.

One became a traitor, another denied his Master, and the rest ran away! But Jesus was not discouraged. He gathered his scattered flock together once more, and even had the temerity to name him who had denied him head of his new foundation.

To be sure the structure and efficacy and indestructibility of the Church cannot be comprehended if one does not see the divine power that works in her. But it is also the work of man, the Man Jesus, and as such it bears witness to his manly greatness and geniality.

Jesus chose men exclusively to be the standard-bearers in his kingdom. Although a circle of faithful women followed him and served him during his public mission, although they held out so bravely beneath his Cross, and were the first messengers of his resurrection, it was, nevertheless, to men he transferred his authority and sacred powers. Admittedly the reason for this preference is to be found primarily in the Jewish tradition, according to which women could not be considered for office in the Church, but there likewise reveals itself in this choice the masculine character in the Church founded by Jesus. Already in the prophetic symbolism of the Old Testament the relation between Christ and Israel was that of a mystical marriage. God in a mystical sense was the bridgeroom and spouse and Israel his bride. This symbol might be used much more aptly to describe the relation of Christ to his Church. He is the bridegroom, and the Church his bride. As his representatives and co-workers the Apostles stand in a similar relationship to the Church; hence they would naturally have to be of the same sex as their master.

CHAPTER III

His Attitude to Woman

I. HIS CONSECRATED VIRILITY

The Son of God took human nature when he became man. That means that all the dispositions and potentialities with which the Creator endowed human nature became his too. In these were included all those dispositions and potentialities by which man is enabled in a special way to share in the creative power of God. He was spiritually and physically a man.

What, then, was the attitude of the man Jesus to sex? What role did it play in his life? What was his fundamental estimation of it? Did sexual relationship affect in any way his personal desires or his social intercourse with women? Such questions as these we shall now turn our attention to, and with due reverence answer them in so far as that is possible.

Out of reverence for his divine person most writers on our Divine Lord have passed these questions over in silence, but reverence does not forbid us to speak of them simply and straightforwardly and to accept in his physical existence all that is not opposed to his divine dignity.

The attitude of Jesus to sex is of the greatest importance, not only for the understanding of his human existence, but in order to judge correctly his redemptive work. Because of original sin the sexual relationships of men were thrown into chaotic confusion. Jesus came to purify, to restore order and to redeem in this as in other spheres of human existence, and his judgement in this matter is decisive.

We shall see this matter in a clearer light if we first consider the attitude adopted by other religious personalities in history to this question of sex. Some there were, who, on purely moral grounds considered the active intercourse of the sexes evil and reprehensible. They struggled against the sexual instinct and tried to exterminate it completely. Others went to the opposite extreme and regarded it as a religious activity. There existed, and still exist, pagan aberrations which are dignified by the name of "holy prostitution." Yet others there were, who, for ascetic reasons, tried to subjugate and forcibly suppress the sexual instinct, to ignore it as if it did not exist. And still others there are who wage a life-long war on it, and strive by every means to bring it into subjection and keep it in order.

But Jesus cannot be included in any of the above categories. In his personal desires and behavior the sexual instinct played no part. Jesus enjoyed an unprecedented freedom, a freedom so perfect that it transcends our understanding, and which we may not question without a very good reason. Since we are speaking of the Man Jesus a consideration of the nature of his freedom is unavoidable.

A study of the life of Jesus affords not the slightest trace of any struggle he might have had to wage in the domain of sex. Jesus neither hates, nor fears, nor despises, nor struggles against the sexual instinct. Nor is there any evidence that he had to keep it in subjection.

There are souls, who, in so far as the life of impulse and instinct is concerned, are practically insensible. They know neither struggle nor the victory consequent thereon and live indifferent to both. Did Jesus belong, perhaps, to this class of persons? By no means! The Being of Jesus is full of a deep warmth. Everything in him lives. Everything is awake and full of creative energy. With what interest he meets men! His love for them is not prompted merely by duty and will, but is a stream flowing from itself, for love is the mainspring of his Being. Nobody whose eyes can see and whose heart is well-disposed will discover in the manifestations of his affection anything in the nature of constraint or compulsion. They are demonstrations of a clear, warm freedom. When we call to mind the image of Jesus we find everything in it rich and palpitating—but with all its energies centered in the heart and forming its motive-power drawn up into his mind and becoming intellectual energy; oriented to God and flowing towards Him in a constant, unending stream. His virility is thoroughly sanctified and dedicated to God.

It is in this that the incomprehensibility of Jesus consists, that the fullness of his energy directs itself to God without violence, compulsion or deception, and again from God to men, and that everything in him is so clear and translucent. From him, whose references to sex were so rare, there emanates a power of assurance, purification, and mastery of these forces, which is unparalleled. This liberty, maturity and integrity of his manhood is not the fruit of any struggle he might have had to wage; it is simply the illumination of his unique, incomparable nature. The manhood which is exemplified in Jesus is that which was embodied in the original creative plan of God in all its splendor and glory.

But would it not bring him nearer to men and make

him more sympathetic towards their failings and encourage them to take him for their model if there were to be found in him any revolt of the senses or the triumph of a victorious struggle, if his maturity and freedom were the reward for victory in that fight which every normal man has to face in greater or lesser degree? Is there not some justification for the objection: "It was easy for him. He had no struggle to make. He had no difficulties to contend with." And does not the revolt of the senses indicate a vitality, which he evidently did not possess? Would his interior life not have gained in richness, depth and beauty if his sensual life had not been so well-ordered and so subordinated? Let us first consider the latter group of questions. It is impossible for us human beings with our darkened understanding and corrupt nature consequent on original sin to form a concept of the sensual life of man in the state of original justice, for fallen man is acquainted with the sensual life only in its disordered state. In itself the activity and depth of the sensual life is a sign of vitality, health and the joy of life, but not the rebellious, disordered cravings of the senses contrary to reason and the inspirations of the guiding spirit. Vitality in its true and full sense is the harmonious activity of the whole person, of his spiritual, intellectual and sensuous life, in such a manner that the activity of the spirit must not be restricted or destroyed by the demands of the intellect and the senses, but, on the contrary, supported and promoted thereby. The intellectual life must be subordinated to the spiritual, and the spirit must have freedom of movement in the realm of the intellect and the senses. Only thus do we achieve a genuinely happy vitality, comprehensive of the whole man. And this is utterly incompatible with any stirrings of the senses against the spirit, hence it is not permissible to interpret such insubordination as a sign of vitality. It would be easy enough also to prove that men of all nations and all classes when faced with momentous decisions and efforts which called for great concentration of energy, took special care to discipline and order their sexual life. Any real appreciation, then, of the sensual life of Jesus must lie outside our experience, but, on the other hand, we must guard against referring to it as "controlled" or "restrained" or "repressed," for that would be to deprive it of its character of spontaneity, originality, integrity and freedom of movement, and consequently of its incomparable beauty.

Would the Man Jesus have gained in natural sympathy if he had been obliged to struggle against rebellious senses? Let us leave out of consideration whether any revolt of the senses would be reconcilable with the sacredness of his person. Theologians would be unanimous in rejecting such a hypothesis. A human being regards any unruly movements of his senses as a weakness and a diminution of his freedom, and involuntarily one is drawn to the person who with interior freedom is master of himself. It is not the fact that this mastery has been gradually won as a result of persevering struggle that impresses, rather it is the mastery itself, the control of the being as an expression of strength and dignity and nobility. It is just this characteristic in the Man Jesus which makes such a striking impression on every normal, healthy person: his interior freedom, his liberty of spirit, his manhood, free from trace of present weakness or past struggle, the embodiment of the power, strength and fullness of perfect, glorious manhood. That which is so constantly and refreshingly surprising and attractive in the Man Jesus is that such an innate, personal abundance of strength and energy and dominion is not only possible but actually present and effective in him. Is he, by reason of his lack of personal experience, incapable of appreciating our interior struggles and difficulties? This question requires no answer for him who believes of the Man Jesus what John the Evangelist writes of him: "He knew them all, and he needed not that any should give testimony of men: for he knew what was in man." *John ii. 25*

Jesus went through life alone. No woman could share his life. In view of the unique character of his being this fact is so self-evident that, generally speaking, we do not even advert to it. The mere thought that a woman should share the life of this man is repugnant to our religious sensibility.

Let us try to find a dogmatic basis for this sense of repugnance. Jesus was the Son of God. From the first moment of its existence his individual human nature was assumed by the second Divine Person. The assumption of human nature by the second Divine Person means that all mankind, the whole of creation, of which human nature is a comprehension and representation, is assumed into God. We speak of a mystical marriage-bond between God and creation in a God-man, Jesus Christ. Hence the human nature of Christ appears before God in the role of a bride. It belongs to God, is completely and exclusively surrendered to God and dedicated to him. The incarnate God himself must in a higher sense be regarded as an essential, mutual marriage. Therefore a further conjugal union of the Man Jesus in the purely human sphere would be absolutely and symbolically impossible.

In this we touch also the deepest roots of priestly celibacy. As a co-worker and representative of Christ the priest is, as it were, the bridegroom of the Church. By his ordination he is mystically wed to the Church, he is dedicated to her, he belongs to her, "taken from among men, he is ordained for men in the things that appertain to God." He is, in a special sense, married to the Church, *Hebrew v. 1* hence a physical marriage would be opposed to his dignity and to the symbolism of his calling. He too, like his Master, must go through life alone, surrendering himself with his whole heart and undivided strength to his lofty vocation.

This celibate life of the man Jesus was not a covert flight from marriage. He did not condemn marriage; on the contrary, he showed his high appreciation of it by his desire to reform it. Always and everywhere, marriage, as a human institution, stood in danger of disruption. This was the case even with the Jewish people. According to the Old Law the man had the right of divorce. It was required of him only that he should send the woman a letter signifying his intention to divorce her. Jesus intervened in this matter in favor of the woman. To the Pharisees, who wished to ensnare him with the question of the permissibility of divorce, he replied: "Moses by reason of the hardness of your heart permitted you to put away your wives: but from the beginning it was not so. And I say to you, that whosoever shall put away his wife, except it be for fornication and shall marry another, committeth adultery; and he that shall marry her *Matt.* that is put away, committeth adultery." Thus Jesus *xix. 8f.* appealed to the original position of mankind as intended by the Creator, and showed that this was the rule, and the law of Moses the exception made necessary by the weakness and sinfulness of men.

The doctors of the law in the time of Jesus quarrelled in trivial ways concerning the grounds on which a man could divorce his wife. Jesus stood far above this theological-juridical dispute. He referred to Genesis, and laid his finger on the place where it is recorded that God created men not merely as a species but as sexual and generic beings, and from this generic unity between man and woman he deduced the unity and indissolubility of marriage. "Have ye not read, that he who made man from the beginning, made them male and female? And he said: For this cause shall a man leave father and mother, and shall cleave to his wife, and they two shall be in one flesh. Therefore now they are not two but one flesh. What therefore God hath joined together, let no man put asunder."

Matt. iv. f.

What sacred gravity, what a high estimation of marriage as a human institution this attitude of Jesus bespeaks! It betrays a warm heart and a kindly disposition. A man who despised marriage would not have spoken thus. His attitude to human life is colored and warmed by the fire of his divinity. In him there is no trace of crabbedness or unsociability, no typical bachelor predilection for whims and fancies; on the contrary, the purity and strength of virginity shines forth in him conjoined with paternal maturity and kindness. It is precisely in this that the same, wholesome attitude to life of the Man Jesus reveals itself.

It has not infrequently been argued against priestly celibacy that the celibate lacks the necessary completion and fulfillment of his manhood, since it is only the woman who can evoke all that is best and deepest in a man and help him to realize himself. The God-given capacity for love, together with the strength it generates and which enables men to live together, is so invaluable that it may not be disregarded without prejudice to the individual and the community.

It is comparatively simple to disprove that assertion. By far the greater number of men are married, and so by far the greater number go through life with a woman at their side. Therefore it is in their power to achieve the wished-for spiritual completion. It is true that the woman can arouse the best in a man, hence one might expect to find among the married the happiest, most harmonious and most spiritually complete lives—and in such numbers as to make themselves felt.

But is it so in actual fact? There are undoubtedly men who find in the woman all that the ideal woman should be to a man. But there are likewise numerous unmarried priests who without woman's help live a perfectly normal life and are as happy in their vocation as it is possible to be here below. And it would be quite incorrect to assert that the absence of a woman at their side leaves anything to be desired in their lives and work. They are creatively fruitful in their activity, and their capacity for love finds its most glorious fulfillment in paternal kindness, mildness and readiness for sacrifice, quite independently of the supposed necessary completion of the "dialogistic" side of their nature.

There is a further point. Is there not today something approaching a "marriage crisis"? Are there not very many "unhappy marriages"? And therefore many men and women who not only do not mutually "complete" but actually impede one another, who not only fail to awaken the deepest and best in one another but actually shatter and choke and annihilate it, and in whose conjugal life the capacity for love, far from unfolding and blossoming, turns to hate and bitterness.

Unfortunately there are as yet no reliable statistics available to show whether the greater percentage of unhappy, thwarted souls is to be found among the ranks of the married or the unmarried. But the fact remains that the objections usually advanced against priestly celibacy are not as sound as they would seem. From a psychological point of view it is easy to raise a storm of protest against the celibacy of the clergy by contrasting an example of an ideal marriage with an unfortunate case of priestly defection. Such a comparison is utterly worthless, since there is no reference to the fundamental principles on which both ways of life are based. It is the worst kind of demagogy, and is often resorted to by opponents of the Catholic priesthood.

There have been innumerable instances throughout the course of the centuries to prove that the celibacy of the priest, by which is meant not merely the unmarried state, but the chaste, abstemious life of a priest, is possible as a healthy masculine, productive way of life, and this has been no more refuted by the proportionally small number of priestly defections, than the matrimonial state is refuted and discredited by the many unhappy marriages.

What St. Jerome says with reference to the command that we love our enemies applies with equal fitness to the example set us by the Man Jesus in this matter of celibacy: Christ commands and recommends not the impossible but the perfect.

2. WHO IS MY MOTHER?

What was the attitude of Jesus to his mother? There has been no lack of suggestions that the relation of Jesus to his mother was not what one would expect it to be, and that on different occasions he adopted a strikingly cool, even harsh, attitude towards her. But if we really enter into the life and character of Jesus as a whole it must strike us as beyond all possibility of doubt that he treated his mother with tenderest love and most childlike respect. This man was on perfectly correct terms with his mother. And it is superfluous to require individual proofs in support of this.

One point, however, must be conceded: the behavior of Jesus in relation to his mother as it is recorded for us in the Gospels presents features, which, to a cursory glance, are strange and difficult to understand.

These we must consider in detail, for they afford us an illuminative glance into the soul of the Man Jesus.

Mary was the loving mother of Jesus. She held him to her bosom, nursed him and nourished him. He was her child. She was privileged to address him as "My Child," and "My Son." He awakened in her all the tenderness of mother-love, not merely in the measure with which other human mothers love their children, for the child Jesus was God's gift to Mary by a grace which passes human comprehension. In him a divine mystery lay hidden. The child constituted her unique and precious treasure and her most sublime distinction. Only as "handmaid of the Lord" was she able to accept the divine gift, ever renewing and throwing open her soul to the floodwaters of inexpressible joy. And she loved God and the child with the undivided strength and the intense fervor of a heart at once virginal and maternal. Only once was there such a son, and once, too, such a mother. Who could attempt to describe and evaluate the sentiments which these two hearts reciprocated? And yet in a perusal of the Gospels we come across a noteworthy fact. The natural relationship of mother and son between Mary and Jesus seems to be absolutely ignored and pushed aside. The evangelists often speak of the "Mother of Jesus." Elizabeth greets her with the reverent question: "Whence is this *Luke* to me, that the mother of my Lord should come to me?" *i. 43* The angel imparts in a dream to Joseph the command: "Arise, and take the child and his mother, and fly into *Matt.* Egypt." But, as far as we can establish, Jesus himself *ii. 13* avoids this form of address. There is not a single instance to be found in the Gospels, where he addressed Mary as "Mother." Not even once during his public mission did he present Mary to the people as his mother, even though there would have been more than one favorable opportunity for doing so. The title "Mother" was such an obvious one, that we cannot help wondering why he omitted it in addressing Mary.

The twelve-year-old Jesus was left behind in the temple in Jerusalem. His parents sought him among relatives and friends for three days. At length they found him in the temple among the doctors of the law. Mary spoke to him: "Child, why hast thou done so to us? Behold, thy father and I have sought thee sorrowing." *Luke ii. 41ff.* What now would have been more natural than that the boy should have answered: "Mother, how is it that you sought me?" But he omits this form of address and replies with the strange counter-question: "How is it that you sought me? Did you not know that I must be about my father's business?"

At the marriage-feast of Cana his mother noticed that the wine threatened to run short. That would have been a painful humiliation to the married couple, so Mary called her son's attention to the fact with the words: "They have no wine." Again one would expect that he *John ii. 3* would have addressed her tenderly, somewhat after the following manner: "Mother, do not worry! God will intervene in some way to help." But by no means! Scripture commentators to the present day have had difficulty with his reply. "Woman," he said, "what is it to me and to thee? My hour is not yet come."

On another occasion as he was teaching in a house and the people crowded around him, he was told: "Behold thy mother and thy brethren stand without, seeking thee." But he answered "Who is my mother, and *Matt. xii. 46ff.* who are my brethren?" And stretching forth his hand towards his disciples, he said: "Behold my mother and my brethren. For whosoever shall do the will of my Father, that is in heaven, he is my brother, and sister, and mother." As if he did not recognize her, and would not acknowledge that she was his mother!

And we read that once when he was surrounded by an admiring crowd, a woman—perhaps she was a mother—raised her voice and called out: "Blessed is the womb that bore thee, and the breast which gave thee suck!" "Happy the mother that bore thee," is what she obviously wished to say. And Jesus? It would almost seem that he was jealous of his own mother, so hastily did he seek to divert attention from her. "Yea, rather blessed are they who hear the word of God, and keep it."

Luke xi. 27

Beneath the Cross on Calvary there stood among other women Mary, his mother. At the moment of his death he addressed her once more. It was his farewell word to her. And is it a word of tenderness, of comfort and of gratitude? Not a bit of it! "Woman, behold thy son." He was referring to the beloved apostle John. Then he turned to the latter with the words: "Behold thy mother." He did not say: "John, look at my mother. She will now be alone. Take care of her." Here again we are confronted with the enigma of Jesus addressing Mary as if she were a stranger, and as if he were more concerned about his favorite Apostle than about his own mother.

John xix. 25

The passages we have quoted admit of no doubt that this behavior of Jesus towards his mother was not something fortuitous and unimportant but a deliberate, deeply-grounded policy. If we carefully consider his replies, we shall be able to discover from them in what this policy consisted. Again and again he returns to the same theme: "that which was his Father's," to the Word of God, which must be heard and obeyed, to the Will of God, which must be done, to "the hour" which must have come. The consciousness of his mission spoke from him, and the urgency of the divine command which had been laid on him. He must and would reveal himself as one who was more than the Son of Mary. He was engaged on his life's work: the manifestation of himself as the Messias and Son of God. In that, too, lay the explanation for his remaining behind in the temple. And there remained to him but very little time for the completion of the task which the Father had committed to him. The man in him was up and doing. The man laboring under the heavy burden of a divine command! His task it was to prove that he had descended from on high. Dared he, then, like an ordinary human being, show tenderness to a human mother? Would he not thereby counteract his self-manifestation, and risk being taken for a mere man rather than the Son of God? Dearly though he loved and treasured his mother, in this work of his vocation, in the carrying out of his Father's will she was in his way, and therefore, he was constrained to ask of her the great sacrifice of withdrawing into the background of his life. His filial heart may have been wrung with pity, but, in loyalty to his mission, he ignored his own pain and hers, because he said: "It must be done." And to such a mother he could confidently suggest this sacrifice, because she would not break under it but grow strong. On Calvary, then, the hour was come when he would hold everything in common with her, and therefore he installed her as mother in his kingdom.

3. HOLY CHIVALRY

The observation of the Man Jesus in his dealings with women is the most beautiful and most delicate aspect of a study of his person. Holy gravity and charming tenderness, becoming reserve and natural ease characterize his behavior towards the weaker sex. His attitude to women is so different, so unique, that in this respect no comparison is possible between him and other men. It is simply the expression of the dignity and warmheartedness of the ineffable, incomprehensible Son of God. Woman has never before or since met a man such as Jesus. And never was man loved with the purity and fervor of devotion with which women loved Jesus.

There is nothing in the public life of Jesus to justify the assumption that he had any special preference for men or women. The message of the Kingdom of God was intended for all mankind, men and women alike. And it was to mankind Jesus spoke, and not to members of either sex. The Beatitudes were meant for all whose interior dispositions fitted them to receive such counsels of perfection with faith and docility. Men were bound by the same moral principles as women. Jesus preached no dual morality, no one-sided, masculine moral code. He showed the same firmness in his demands, the same earnestness, the same benevolence towards men and women. And the same invitation was extended to both sexes: "Come to me *all* . . .!" The more weary and heavy laden, the more needy the soul, the more eagerly did Jesus receive him. Purity of intention was the one essential condition.

Men and women alike experienced the healing power of his miracles. To mention only a few of the miracles he worked on women, he cured the mother-in-law of Peter, praised the faith of the Canaanite woman and cured her daughter from a distance. He took pity on the woman suffering from an issue of blood, whom medical skill had failed to relieve, and on her who had been infirm for eighteen years. To the weeping widow of Naim he gave back her only son and he restored the daughter of Jairus to life. He expelled seven evil spirits from the Magdalen, and liberated many other women besides from the bonds of Satan. For he had come to redeem both sexes, and would be a Savior to all the children of Adam.

Side by side with his Apostles we find women in

closest companionship with Christ. The texts in St. *Luke*
Luke's Gospel where this is referred to are not in- *viii. ff.*
frequently overlooked, and so interpreted as if only men
were to be found in his immediate neighborhood. And
yet it is stated expressly: He travelled through the cities
and towns, preaching and evangelizing the kingdom of
God; and the twelve with him. And certain women who
had been healed of evil spirits and infirmities: Mary who
is called Magdalen, out of whom seven devils were gone
forth, and Joanna the wife of Chusa, Herod's steward,
and Susanna, and many others who ministered unto
him of their substance. Indeed, we learn here that he
allowed even women he had cured of possession to attach
themselves to him, a privilege which, ordinarily speaking,
was not accorded to men. We find him *tête-à-tête* with
the man Nicodemus, but also with the Samaritan
woman at the Well of Jacob. To be sure, he received the
man by night in a private house; with the woman he
spoke in the open at a well to which many people came.
All experienced the soothing touch of his pardon and
mercy, not only men, but women, and even such women
as the unknown "great sinner," the adulteress and very
many others whose stories have not been recorded. We
find him accepting invitations to meals from men and
women, and it would appear that he was linked with the
family at Bethany by bonds of the most intimate friend-
ship. "Now Jesus loved Martha, and her sister Mary,
and Lazarus," says John the evangelist.   *John*

In his relations with women did Jesus adapt himself *xi. 5*
to the local manners and customs? It goes without saying
that he did so. That is apparent from the fact that even
his most violent opponents found nothing to reproach
him with in this respect. They denounced and calum-
niated him without mercy, but they never dared to call in
question the decorum and purity of his intercourse with

women. On the other hand, it is interesting to observe the astonishment of the Apostles on the rare occasions when the Master permitted himself to make an exception to the rule. At the well of Jacob, on finding him *tête-à-tête* with the Samaritan woman, they wondered that he talked with her, and it was only their reverence that restrained them from asking: "What seekest thou? Or why talkest thou with her?"

John iv. 7ff.

In the fundamental estimation of man and woman Jesus acknowledged no difference. He accepted both as complete human personalities, but he perfectly understood how to make allowance for the differences in the character of both sexes. How different is his approach to Nicodemus and to the Samaritan woman! His conversation with Nicodemus from the very first sentence takes an objective, a theological turn: "Amen, amen I say to thee, unless a man be born again he cannot see the Kingdom of God." From the woman on the other hand he first requests a friendly service: "Give me to drink!" And in her reply the woman at once adopts a highly personal note: "How dost thou, being a Jew, ask of me to drink, who am a Samaritan woman?" Whereupon Jesus answers her in such a way that her curiosity is aroused and the personal note further emphasized: "If thou didst know the gift of God, and who he is that saith to thee, Give me to drink; thou perhaps would have asked of him, and he would have given thee living water." The rather long conversation remains thus on the personal level, and reaches its climax and conclusion with the self-revelation of Jesus: "I am he (i.e. the Messias) who am speaking with thee."

John iv. 27

John iii. 3ff.

The women in the immediate neighborhood of Jesus stand completely under the veil of modest retirement. He has never brought them into the foreground. Had St. Luke not left us his short testimony, we should probably live in ignorance of the fact that women were to be found among the most intimate followers of Jesus. They are not sent to preach; they play no part in the working of miracles; they are unnamed and unnoticed. Their privilege it was "to minister unto him of their substance," and that is all we know of them. Among his apostles he would not tolerate feminine tutelage or interference of any kind whatever, as the mother of the twin sons had to learn. "She came to him with her sons, adoring and asking something of him. Who said to her: What wilt thou? She saith to him: Say that these my two sons may sit, the one on thy right hand, and the other on thy left, in thy kingdom. And Jesus answering, said: "You know not what you ask. . . ." And he dismissed her with the words: "to sit on my right or left hand is not mine to give to you, but to them for whom it is prepared by my Father." This woman was one of the Galilean women who had followed Jesus.

Matt. xx. 20ff.

The delicate appreciation Jesus had of the impulses of the feminine nature is shown in the two anointings which he accepted from womanly hands. The first of these two instances is related for us in detail by St. Luke in the seventh chapter of his Gospel. In straightforward, classical style, he draws the contrast between the behavior of the hard, self-righteous man Simon and the tender proof of love given by the woman. And the final words of the Gospel narrative illustrate the divine magnanimity with which Jesus rewarded her little gesture: "Thy faith hath made thee safe, go in peace." With what indescribable happiness these words must have filled the soul of the Magdalen, not only because he had pardoned her sins, but, above all, because he had received her, "the sinner," before all the guests, and permitted her to give expression to her great repentance, gratitude and love in a womanly way.

Luke vii. 50

The second anointing is recorded by three of the evangelists, and on reading their accounts of the occurrence one can almost perceive the aroma of the precious spikenard which "filled the whole house." There is such a delicate touch about the whole thing! But here also, at least in St. Matthew's account, the contrast between the masculine reaction and the tender love of the woman is clearly perceptible. "When Jesus was in Bethania in the house of Simon the leper, there came to him a woman having an alabaster-box of precious ointment, and poured it on his head as he was at table." John elaborates a little, it was "a pound of ointment of right spikenard, of great price," and with it she "anointed the feet of Jesus, and wiped his feet with her hair: and the house was filled with the odour of the ointment." "And the disciples seeing it, had indignation, saying: To what purpose is this waste? For this might have been sold for much and given to the poor." They murmured, and criticized, and did not understand. Not so the Man Jesus! He understood and pleaded in her defense: "Why do you trouble this woman? for she hath wrought a good work upon me. For the poor you have always with you; but me you have not always. For she in pouring this ointment upon my body, hath done it for my burial. Amen I say to you, wheresover this Gospel shall be preached in the whole world, that also which she hath done, shall be told for a memory of her." Thus he honored and blessed the contemplative Mary, who already at an early visit of the Master had sat at his feet and listened to his words. In a different way, but equally in conformity with the woman's nature, he blessed and honored the sister Martha, who, it would appear, was the older of the two and ran the house. "She received him into her house," and "was busy about much serving." At the second visit likewise we learn that "Martha served."

Matt.
xxvi. 6ff.

Luke
x. 38f.

Jesus would neither make a Martha of Mary, nor a Mary of Martha, and so he pleaded the cause of Mary who sat at his feet, and honored Martha by accepting her services. And in this consisted the highest distinction and the greatest joy of her life, that it was her privilege to serve the Lord.

CHAPTER IV

Man Before God

I. HIS CONCEPT OF GOD

How did the Man Jesus represent the infinite God to himself? What did he think of Him? What mind did he ascribe to Him? Of what did he prefer to speak when he was occupied with Him? What attribute did he especially emphasize? These and similar questions we shall consider in the following pages.

As man, Jesus was strongly impressed by the transcendence and sovereignty of God. In this respect his concept of God resembles that of the Old Testament, particularly that of the Prophets and Psalmist. It is sparkling with light and color. To him God is the one, unique Lord of mankind. In his mouth the opening words of the formal Jewish creed, the liturgical morning and evening prayer, take on a peculiarly original and vigorous tone: "Hear, O Israel, the Lord, our God, is the only God." God stands alone in sacred Majesty above all things created. He is the Omnipotent, the Primary Cause, the Eternal, He who "hath life in himself." "God is Spirit" the essence of all goodness and grandeur. He is the Unattainable. "Why asketh thou me concerning good? One is good, God." Christ ascribes to

John v. 26

Him all the attributes expressive of power and greatness *Matt.* and beauty and pre-eminence. He calls Him the All- *xix. 17* holy, the Holy One, the Just One, the True One, the All-knowing, from whom nothing is hidden, to whom all secrets are known.

God is the Creator and "Lord of heaven and earth" *Matt.* essentially differing from the world; He is not only the *xi. 25* Source of its mysterious energy, or a mental concept such as the "universe," not merely its nebulous foundation or background, not merely "the Divine"—Jesus never once used this expression—but the living, personal God, to whom we pray, whom we address as "thou," who possessed existence and reality even before the world was. He created the world; it is His work, His property, His vineyard. As Lord of it He has something to say in it; indeed, His is the final word. Heaven is His throne, the earth His foot-stool, and Jerusalen His kingly city.

Before this sublime Lord the Man Jesus bowed not from any interior compulsion, or out of a sense of cold-blooded duty or in slavish fear, but quite consciously and of his own free will. His soul opened up automatically, as it were; he lived absolutely in the presence of God and stood always and everywhere in interior readiness and holy watchfulness before Him. The Will of God constituted the norm of his life, the ever urgent concern which claimed all his energy. He knew nothing greater, more glorious or more important, than the abandonment of himself, with all the strength of his manly will and the fervor of his loving heart to this God. To the Scribe who asked him "which was the first commandment of *Mark* all," he replied: "The first commandment of all is . . . *xii. 29* thou shalt love the Lord thy God with thy whole heart, with thy whole soul, and with thy whole mind and with thy whole strength."

The Man Jesus did not conceive God as an inactive

Being throned in indolent, inaccessible majesty somewhere beyond the clouds, and utterly indifferent to the
world of men, not as a "God of the dead, but of the liv-
Mark ing," as a God of stupendous creative energy and all-
xii. 27 embracing activity. How could he who lived for work
and activity conceive of God as an inactive Being? How
could he have prayed the Psalms and read the Prophets
without the firm conviction of a creatively effectual God,
who was deeply concerned for the world. "My Father
John worketh until now," he said. All movement, all life, all
v. 17 growth originated from His creative energy. He it is who
causes the sun to shine and the rain to fall. He nourishes
the birds of the air, and clothes the lilies of the field. He
takes thought for the sparrow on the house-top, and
every hair of our head is present to His all-seeing eye.
Before Him the destinies of men unfold themselves in the
power of His efficacious strength. He gives the daily
bread, preserves from temptation, delivers from evil, and
distributes rewards and punishments according to the
deserts of men. All religious and supernatural life is inspired by Him. He is the author of all sanctity and integrity, of all revelation and illumination, of all faith and
all union with God. He sends the Redeemer, Christ, and
the Comforter, the Holy Ghost, He creates the moral
order and busies Himself with its complete realization
"Will not God revenge his elect who cry to him day and
night: and will he have patience in their regard? I say
Mark to you that he will quickly revenge them." God promises
xviii. 6 to reward the good; the evil-doers He threatens with
destruction; all alike He summons once to judgment.
Even for every idle word He demands an account, but
the glass of water given in His Name to the fellow-man
goes not unrewarded.

The God of the Man Jesus is not only a Lord God,
but a Father-God. "Father" is the form of address which

Jesus most often uses in reference to God. It has even
been said that the essential point in the message of Jesus
was the manifestation of the Fatherhood of God, but this
is to take too narrow and one-sided a view of the Gospel
of Christ. This, however, is true: by his steady, confident
acknowledgement of God as Father Jesus leaves far
behind the pagan and Jewish concept of the First Person.
The only formal prayer he has left to us begins with a
salutation to God as Father, and nobody ever prayed so
earnestly to the heavenly Father as he did. The majesty,
immensity, power and transcendence of God did not
crush and oppress him; rather did he interpret these attributes as power to help, to uplift and to pity. The God
of Jesus so loved the world and men that he gave his *John iii. 16f.*
only-begotten son "that whosoever believeth in him, may
not perish, but may have life everlasting. For God sent
not his Son into the world, to judge the world, but that *Luke vi. 38*
the world may be saved by him." He is a generous God
who is ready to give "good measure and pressed down *Luke xv. 20*
and shaken together and running over." He is the Father
of the prodigal son, who, catching sight of the returning
sinner while he is yet a long way off, being moved with
compassion, runs to him and falls upon his neck and
kisses him, and who brings forth the first robe, and puts it
on him, and puts a ring on his hand and shoes on his
feet. He is the God who says "there shall be joy in heaven
upon one sinner that doth penance, more than upon *Luke xv. 7*
ninety-nine just who need not penance." Finally one
might designate the God, whom Jesus preached and
loved with all the strength of his heart, as the God of
great missions. By this God Jesus knew himself to have
been sent and called to the greatest and most sublime
task of all, that of redeeming and sanctifying mankind
and establishing the kingdom of God. This God has

confidence in the human being, He harnesses His forces and assigns him mighty tasks.

He will not permit man to bury his talent in the earth; He will not allow the tree to remain barren. He is the husbandman who will take away every branch that *John* beareth not fruit, "and every one that beareth fruit he *xv. 2ff.* will purge it, that it may bring forth more fruit." He is the heavenly Father who will be glorified if men achieve great things.

If we sum up in a final survey what Jesus in his teaching, preaching and parables has made known to us about God we get a picture somewhat as follows: God is an infinite, personal transcendent Being, sovereign, spiritual and omnipotent. And He seeks "true adorers who will *John* adore him in spirit and in truth." *iv. 23*

This God is not enthroned at inaccessible distance somewhere beyond the clouds in complacent and inactive self-sufficiency. His existence is all life; he is intimately concerned in the world; his Love belongs to men. What we learn of Him sounds like an urgent summons to sin-laden, timorous, hesitating mankind to cast off all fear and take courage, not to remain pressed to the earth in the hopelessness of despair, but to stand upright and breathe once more, to rejoice and to feel free. It is a distinct appeal to men to throw open their hearts to receive all the riches intended for them, and to set out boldly and courageously for the goal, which He will certainly enable them to reach. For this God will have no slaves, no wage-earners, no mere subjects, but dearly beloved children who with genuine confidence look up and call him Father. Nor will he have men who with sighs and groans drag their tortured way through the valley of tears, but fresh, energetic, happy, self-confident beings who in the strength of His helping grace go bravely on their way.

The God of the Man Jesus is the God, not only of the contemplative, but of the active life, not only the God of the theologian, but likewise of the poor and the simple; of the penitent sinner as of the canonized saint; the God not only of individual hearts but of the whole human race. Before him only the cowardly, the ambitious, the self-righteous need stand in awe, for on them falls the full rigor of his Justice; against them is enkindled the consuming fire of His Anger. For them, if they persist in their impenitence, there is ready the exterior darkness, where there is eternal weeping and futile gnashing of teeth. But for the pure of heart, and for those of goodwill his last word will be: "Come, ye blessed . . . enter into the joy of the Lord."

And so the characteristic features of this concept of God are greatness and immensity. A real, existent God stands before us, and not a mere elusive phantom of the mind experienced only in fleeting momentary moods; a God full of life and intensity, but free from all softness and sentimentality; a God of severity despite His infinite goodness: a manly, and yet a thoroughly paternal God, in short, a God, as only a man like Jesus could see, and know and make Him known.

2. HIS PIETY

There was perfect conformity between the piety which the Man Jesus practiced in his own personal life and that which he preached and recommended to others. And since his preaching sprang from his personal piety, consideration of the content of his preaching will enable us to establish the nature of his piety. The prayers which have come down to us from his own mouth, in particular, afford us a most informative insight into the peculiar quality of his interior, spiritual life.

Many such prayers have been recorded for us, prayers

which expressed his own personal needs and desires, and the prayer which he recommended as a model to his Apostles. The so-called "high-priestly prayer," that magnificent out-pouring of his soul to his heavenly Father in the supper-room, will serve as an example of the former type of prayer, and the "Our Father" of the latter. The one represents his personal prayer to the heavenly Father, spoken directly before the beginning of his Passion, in an hour of the deepest emotion and inward tension. The other was expressly composed by him for general use among his Apostles and followers of all times. Nevertheless both prayers show definite, common characteristics, and indeed markedly masculine features. In them we hear a man praying, not merely in the speaker, but in the content and form of the prayer and this despite the fact that the Pater Noster is the classical formula of prayer for all mankind, women as well as men. Still we believe that we can prove the truth of the assertion that this prayer quite obviously bears the stamp of the masculine mind, and even had it originated from a woman it would be described as a strong, manly prayer.

In the first chapter of St. Luke's Gospel there is recorded for us a woman's prayer. When Mary visited her cousin Elizabeth and saw what the Holy Ghost had wrought in her, she was herself moved by the Holy Spirit, and she broke forth into ecstatic prayer of jubilation to which she gave formal expression in the Magnificat. If we compare the two prayers of Jesus with the prayer of Mary it will at once be obvious that Jesus really prayed in a masculine way, while Mary's prayer is a true expression of her feminine nature.

The author of the Pater Noster and the high-priestly prayer begins with a clear, definite orientation of his spirit away from himself to God and objective facts:

"Our Father who art in Heaven . . ." "Father, the hour is come. . . ."

Then he occupies himself with God: His essence, the sanctification of His Name, His glorification, His activity, His kingdom. And even where Christ refers to himself, he sees himself as one who belongs to God: "Glorify thy *John* Son, so that thy Son may glorify Thee." *xvii. 1*

The woman prays otherwise. She knows, to be sure, that she is in the presence of God, but her glance appears to be directed to herself. It is of herself that she speaks, of the state and activity of her soul, of God as her Salvation, of the great things He has done for her soul, and of what will be done for her in the future.

In the prayer of the Man Jesus the "thou" and "thine" predominate; in that of the woman the "my" and "me." The prayer of the man sounds objective, impersonal, sharp, pregnant with thought and directed into the distance; even the purpose of being is touched upon: "This is eternal life: that they may know thee, the only *John* true God, and Jesus Christ, whom thou hast sent." The *xvii. 3* woman's prayer, on the other hand, is subjective and personal; it is expressive of the mood of her own soul, sees the immediate and the proximate, and is confined to her own experiences. The man speaks of what is to happen, of work and activity: "I have finished the work *John* which thou gavest me to do. . . ." The woman concen- *xvii. 4* trates on what she has actually received, on her person, on what God intends to do for her—hers is a concrete approach to prayer. Granted that she, too, speaks of the power and might of God: "His Mercy is from genera- *Luke* tion to generation. . . . He hath showed might in his *i. 50* arm . . .," her first thought nevertheless is for what God has done in her. The man, likewise, includes in his prayer his personal desires: "Give us this day our daily bread, forgive us our trespasses . . .," "for them do I pray," "all my things are thine, and thine are mine: and I am glorified in them," but only after he has spoken of the great essential, the desire of God and his work of Salvation.

Thus the external form and the interior structure of the prayer of Jesus testify to the masculine nature of his piety. This is especially clear from the comparison with the manner of prayer of Mary, but it is still more evident from the content of the prayers he formulated himself. Let us now turn to a consideration of the Pater Noster. Simplicity, clarity and liberality characterize the piety which speaks from that great prayer; and yet it is a prayer of monumental proportions. It is concerned with the great elementary desires of mankind; their relations with God and their own earthly needs, the "daily bread" which includes all the necessaries of body, health, employment, etc., and of soul, such as the need for pardon of sin, and the great fundamental grace of final repentance. The same simplicity and charity of soul speaks from the "high-priestly prayer." Here, likewise the emphasis is on the great essentials: the glorification of the Father through and in his Son, the knowledge of God, the work of redemption, the faith and the salvation of men, the unity of the faithful in Christ. "I have glorified thee on the earth: I have finished the work which thou gavest me to do: And now glorify thou me, O Father, with myself, with the glory which I had, before the world was, with thee." That is the kernel of this prayer. Everything else, even the prayer for his own, is related to the accomplishment of the one mighty work of redemption, and the glorification of the Father by him who was sent.

John xvii. 4ff.

Such was the piety of Jesus: simple and clear. There is no trace of anxiety or confusion. Such a prayer could never emanate from a "complex soul," or from a mean

or narrow-minded person. In such piety as this breadth
and freedom of spirit, order and peace of soul are the
predominant features. Trivial requests prompted by
egoism, fear, or distrust find no place in it; all personal
and worldly desires, which should also be presented to
God in prayer, are included, subordinated and expressed
in the supremely-great, divinely-important petitions: that
the Will of God may be done, that the kingdom of God
may come and flourish, that God may be glorified in
everything, that men may be saved from want and
damnation: "Those whom thou gavest me have I kept: *John
and none of them is lost, but the son of perdition, that xvii. 12*
the Scripture may be fulfilled." "Thy Will be done on
earth, as it is in Heaven." Such prayer breathes supernal
calm, straightforward thought, firm Will, and infinite
circumspection in the setting up of man's goal. In the
soul of him who prayed thus there must have reigned the
infinite peace of God, that peace which he would be-
queath to his own. It is the same calm and peace and
beauty which speaks to us from the parables of Jesus.

From the Pater Noster, then, there is wafted towards
us the fresh breath of a deep and solid piety. The prayer
distinctly rotates on a central pivot, the one thing necessary, God and the abandonment of mankind to Him.
The whole first part of the prayer is concerned with:
"Hallowed be thy Name, thy Kingdom come, thy Will *Matt.
be done on earth as it is in Heaven." In a similar way vi. 9*
the high-priestly prayer turns on the glorification of the
Father, on the salvation of the disciples, and on everlasting life. "I pray not that thou shouldst take them out *John
of the world, but that thou shouldst keep them from xvii. 15*
evil."

Thus, in all his preaching and teaching, the piety of
Jesus centered around this one great essential, and
wherever he found that the glad tidings of the Gospel

had, by the Grace of God, taken root in human hearts,
his joy found expression in ecstatic prayer: "I confess to
thee, O Father, Lord of Heaven and earth because thou
hast hid these things from the wise and prudent, and
hast revealed them to little ones." And to his Apostles he
said: "Rejoice not in this that spirits are subject unto
you: but rejoice in this, that your names are written in
Heaven." "Yea, rather blessed are they who hear the
word of God and keep it." "What shall it profit a man,
if he gain the whole world, and suffer the loss of his
soul?"

Matt. xi. 25

Luke x. 20
Mark viii. 36

There we have genuine, manly piety, which knows
how to distinguish between the important and unimportant, the essential and inessential. For piety does not consist in empty emotionalism or in striking achievements or
even in miracles, or in the saying of "Lord, Lord" but in
the determined, unconditional acceptance of the
sovereignty of God.

That means, of course, that we must be prepared to
"drink the chalice" with Christ, and to "take up our
Cross daily, and follow him." Yea, even when higher
things are at stake, we must not hesitate to "cut off the
hand" and "pluck out the eye." It was this piety which
enabled the Man Jesus to deliver himself to the death of
the Cross, in obedience to the Will of God, in order, by
his sacrificial death, to glorify the Father and to effect
the redemption of mankind.

But in spite of its depth and austerity the piety of Jesus
was full of sincerity, tenderness and cordiality. In this
naturally his mysterious relationship to the Father plays
its part, but this interior sense of the proximity of God
does not rule out his human and masculine susceptibilities, rather it enhances and transfigures them. The reverence and worship, surrender and love of the divine Son
palpitated towards the Father from a human heart. The

Father in Heaven was the living reality in which the soli-
tude of this man was resolved. There he felt himself
secure; there he felt at home. Thence he drew the supernatural strength for his task, and there in fruitful intercourse with the Father he found that appeasement and
companionship which he, too, needed in his solitary way
of life. In proof of this we have his own oft-repeated
words: "I am not alone." "Behold the hour cometh, and *John*
it is now come, that you shall be scattered every man to *viii. 16*
his own, and shall leave me alone: and yet I am not *xvi. 32*
alone, because the Father is with me." Karl Adam says
that the prayer of Jesus "is nothing but a constant keeping in touch with the Father, a blessed constraint to
resolve the loneliness of his 'I' in the 'Thou' of the
Father. It is in prayer that he achieves a union with the
Father in which none other, not even his Apostles, may
participate."

In the piety of Jesus there is a thoroughly man-like
quality of virile modesty and reserve, for the man is not
ostentatious in his piety. By this obviously is not intended
that timidity and reserve which originates from cowardice
and human respect, but that which marks the masculine
character. "When thou shalt pray, enter into thy cham-
ber, and having shut the door, pray to thy Father in
secret," was Jesus' command to his Apostles, and that *Matt.*
precept was certainly supported by his own example. He *vi. 6*
never paraded his piety, and sharply condemned all
hypocrisy in others: "And when ye pray, you shall not
be as the hypocrites, that love to stand and pray in the
synagogues and corners of the streets, that they may be
seen by men: Amen I say to you, they have received their
reward." He rejected, likewise, the mere babbling of *Matt.*
prayers, and lip-service which characterized the prayer *vi. 5ff.*
of the heathens who "think that in their much speaking
they may be heard," and required of his followers that

they worship "in spirit and in truth." Therefore, we are not surprised to find in the Gospels that Jesus went into a lonely place to pray, or up into a mountain alone, or that he spent the whole early morning or night in prayer, for this hankering after seclusion found its source in his masculine nature. But there were occasions when he made no secret of his prayer, when, indifferent to witnesses, he prayed in the presence of his disciples or of the people silently, or, according to Jewish custom, aloud. For he was no slave to human respect.

His piety was always discreet and related to life. He never gave the impression of a religious oddity. He had nothing in common with the ascetic or hermit in the accepted sense of the word, and this constitutes a fundamental difference between his piety and that of John the Baptist whose external appearance as an ascetic and preacher of penance was in the manner of the old prophets. There is nothing more alien to the character of Jesus than the attitude which is familiarly known as bigotry. There is a refreshing austerity about it, but for all its interior quality it nevertheless remains orientated to life and the world. We find him engaged in strenuous work the whole day through, and always ready to receive kindly the crowds who thronged about him. All were most highly edified by him and felt themselves urged to sanctity, and yet there stood before them, as it were, just an ordinary busy man. His exhortations never sounded importunate or exaggerated or artificial or spurious. What he spoke and preached was invariably self-evident, illuminative and convincing, even when he was making the highest moral demands. He preached piety impressively, without too much external insistence on it. His life and work were edifying in the truest and most beautiful sense of the word. His work was the external expression of his prayer and piety, that work which was the

will and command of his Father. The same attitude to
work which stamped his life as a carpenter in Nazareth
was the distinguishing mark of his public activity.

There were times, nevertheless, when Jesus interrupted
work and devoted himself quite deliberately and exclusively to works of religion and devotional exercises. He
prayed before and after meals, on the Sabbath day he
attended divine services in the synagogue, he celebrated
the religious festivals of his people, he commanded him
whom he had healed of leprosy to make the prescribed
offering, he acknowledged the authority of religious
superiors: "All things whatsoever they shall say to you, *Matt.*
observe and do: but according to their works do ye not." *xxiii. 3*
He often betook himself quite openly to prayer, and
devoted hours, whole nights, and even weeks to it. Moreover, since the work-filled day left him very little leisure
for prayer, he dedicated the early morning hours or the
late evening to it. Particularly before important decisions
he prayed long and earnestly. Thus it was that he spent
the whole night in prayer before choosing his Apostles;
likewise before his last journey to Jerusalem when he
ascended Mount Thabor and was transfigured, and during the last sad days before his Passion he withdrew into
the Garden of Gethsemane to pray.

How magnificently the Man Jesus stood before his
God. So upright and open, so firmly confident and yet so
reverent and so humble! He bowed willingly before God,
because he knew that such a gesture did not humiliate
but strengthen and restore order and give freedom in
man's inner life.

3. HIS PHILOSOPHY

The Man Jesus did not live as a hermit in a desert. He
stood in the midst of life, dealt with many men, was a
child of his times and his people, was drawn daily into

innumerable conversations and initiated into the views and judgments, into the hopes and fears of the people. In the writings of the Old Testament were recorded the stupendous events in the history of his people, and on each Sabbath he heard an extract read therefrom.

He was familiar with the political conditions of his time, his people, and his homeland. He knew who the Romans were and what their domination signified. He was confronted by life and the world as power-factors which compelled him to consider and adopt a definite, personal point of view. The keenness and vivacity of his disposition would indicate that he did not present an indifferent and unsympathetic front to what was happening around him. He, too, had what is called a philosophy of life: a definite, ultimate attitude to the world as a whole, a comprehensive, personal judgment on the nature and worth, the meaning and destiny of the world and world-events.

What was his attitude to the world? What did he think of it? Did he consider it good or evil? Innocuous or mysterious? Hateful or desirable? The effort to answer these and similar questions leads us to a consideration of the philosophy of the Man Jesus.

In the teaching of Jesus we seek in vain for any peculiar utterances of a scientific or philosophic nature concerning the external form or the internal structure of the universe. Cosmology, as a science, formed no part of the body of revelation which it was his task to interpret for men. In so far as his references to the destruction of the world presuppose a definite, scientific cosmos, it is based on expressions and descriptions from the Old Testament and the accepted views of his time. That was a cosmology based on the outward visible appearances of things and true in so far as it went. He simply accepted this view without questioning its ultimate scientific truth.

His theory of the universe is based not on profane science but on religion. This is evidenced by the fact that in his references to the world as the universe and essence of all things created, he systematically avoided the use of the profane and pagan-sounding expression "cosmos," then in general use in contemporary literature, and employed instead the term "heaven and earth" sanctified by biblical tradition and liturgical usage. "I confess to thee, O Father, Lord of Heaven and Earth," by which he meant Lord of the whole world and the whole universe. "Heaven and earth shall pass away." "Till heaven and earth pass, one jot, or one tittle shall not pass of the law, till all be fulfilled."

Jesus considered the world not as nature in the philosophical sense of the word, but as a creature indebted for its existence to the creative will and word of an omnipotent God. It was with the relation of the word to God, as its Creator, Lord, Judge and Redeemer that he was especially concerned. In his philosophy there was no such thing as nature existing independently of God, and therefore he is no nature-lover in the sense of a natural enthusiasm or purely sensible surrender to it. Perhaps the best way to interpret Christ's conception of the world is as the stage and field of action for God's redemptive dealings with men, for this notion is peculiarly his own and is not met with either in paganism or Judaism.

Mark xiii. 31
Matt. v. 18

According to the declaration of Jesus the existence of the world is limited by an absolute beginning and an absolute end. He repeatedly refers to the "first beginning" and the "foundation" of the world, and is thoroughly acquainted with the opening sentence of the Scriptures: "In the beginning God created heaven and earth." The longest and most terrifying discourse of his dealt with the end of the world. Between the beginning and the end this "aeon" must expire, that is this transient,

elusive world of time, then will come the "other world,"
the "future aeon" of everlasting duration. The world
runs its course once, and once only. Any theory of the
recurrence of things and worlds is in direct contradiction
to the philosophy of Jesus. Only once does the rich man
of the parable enjoy this earthly life. Then he dies. And
there is no return.

The world understood as the universe and essence of
all creation, as the dwelling-place of a man and the stage
of history, Jesus considered and accepted as the work of
the creative power of God.

He looked on it as God's property, penetrated and
governed by His life-giving power and ordaining energy.
Thus it was proclaimed by the prophets, thus it stood in
the psalms, thus it was embodied in the texts of prayer
for daily use and for the great festivals: "God doth according to his will, as well with the powers of heaven as
among the inhabitants of the earth; and there is none
that can resist his hand and say to him: why hast thou
Dan. done it?" All creatures owe their existence to God, men
iv. 32 in a special manner; to him they are responsible; to
glorify him is their purpose in life, "that they may glorify
the Father who is in heaven."

Because he regarded the world as the work and property of the Father in heaven, and was convinced that
God "lovest all things that are and hatest none of the
Wisdom things which he has made," Jesus, too, loved the world.
xi. 25 His manner of referring to the lilies of the field, the
sparrows on the house-tops, the raven in the field, seeds,
and growth and the blossoming and ripening of corn
bespeaks the great benevolence with which he approached all being, and throws special light on his
familiarity with nature, which he looked upon as the
image of God and the symbol of his attributes, and

therefore the symbol and bearer of higher truths and realities.

The world as the theater of God's redemptive activity appeared to him as a mighty field in which the seed of God's word was set and should send forth fruit. To be sure he did not close his eyes to the fact that the divine seed can fall on many kinds of soil: some on hard ground, others on unproductive rock, still others among thorns, and some on good ground where it brings forth fruit in abundance. Undoubtedly there will be weeds among the wheat, but God permits his sun to shine peacefully "on good and bad, just and unjust."

What was the place of suffering in the philosophy of Jesus? The Man of Nazareth proposed no philosophic theory of the origin and meaning of suffering in the world. He simply accepted it as a fact and gave it a new depth of meaning. But before considering it more thoroughly let us see how Jesus reacted to the suffering he encountered in his immediate surroundings, in order to obtain a clearer view of his fundamental conception of this great mystery.

He did not in any way evade it; nor did he ignore it, or under-estimate it, or deny it. He was not raised above it by religious fanaticism or mystical enthusiasm, or in any way unbalanced by it. He opened his arms to all who came to him bent under their burden of sorrow and suffering; he even commanded them to come to him: "Come to me all ye that labour and are heavy-burdened, and I will refresh you." He felt quite equal to the load of human suffering and want, but we have no single word of his to show that he had any intention of expunging suffering in the world. If we try to interpret the actions of Jesus as a "caritative activity" we perceive immediately that his practical approach to suffering was quite unique and different from the prophylactic, mitigating, con-

Matt.
xi. 28

soling approach of Charity, as it is practiced today, and highly though we may appreciate this Charity, we are nevertheless compelled to acknowledge that it has nothing in common with the actions of Jesus. Something quite different takes place here. There is no question of social or economic measures to check and relieve the want and sorrow of mankind. He saw much deeper and struck at the roots of the problem. That brings us to a consideration of the interpretation which Jesus gave to suffering, an interpretation which is immediately related to his philosophy.

In the eyes of Jesus the world is by no means innocent and inoffensive. He saw it in a pitiable state, estranged from its Creator and Lord, torn by sin, and having become the adversary of God under the dominion of the "princes of this world." Because of sin and disorder the world stands judged by God. According to the prophetical utterances of the Old Testament the divine Judge will pour the vials of his wrath on the sinful world at the end of time. Jesus knew more than that. His appearance marked the beginning of the end. The great judgment was already at hand. The suffering and sorrow of the world are nothing but the operation and execution of this mysterious judgment which overtakes innocent and guilty alike, if with very different meaning. His own Passion and death were but the initial stage of this judgment which he, as representative of mankind, wished to take on himself, in a spirit of obedience and expiation, thereby identifying himself with man's distress and revealing its true and ultimate significance. Thus he spoke to the weeping women on the way to Calvary: "Daughters of Jerusalem, weep not over me, but weep for yourselves and for your children. For behold the days shall come wherein they will say: Blessed are the barren, and the wombs that have not borne, and the paps that have

Luke xxiii. 28

not given suck. Then shall they begin to say to the mountains: Fall upon us; and to the hills; cover us. For if in the green wood they do these things, what shall be done in the dry?" He himself was the "green wood," the innocent, vicarious victim for the sins of men; the "dry wood" are those sinners who persist in their impenitence, and who will undergo a far more severe judgment.

Pain and want and distress are inevitable in a world, which has fallen under the domination of the "princes of this world," and become inimical to God, and hence *Luke* constantly delivered up to judgment. The good, the ad- *23, 28* herents of Christ, the "children of light" though not indeed of this world, must nevertheless live in it "till the harvest-time." And they will experience distress and suffering till they enter into the kingdom of God: "You shall lament and weep, but the world shall rejoice: and you shall be made sorrowful but your sorrow shall be turned into joy. A woman, who when she is in labour, hath sorrow, because her hour is come: but when she hath brought forth the child, she remembereth no more the anguish, for joy that a man is born into the world. So *John* also you now indeed have sorrow." For the wicked, the *xii. 20ff.* unbelievers, and the impenitent, the suffering and distress of this world are but the beginning of their final rejection by God.

Therefore according to the conception of Jesus the sufferings of the world had a temporal character. They are inseparable from the Christian existence; they have a special meaning in the history of salvation. Life here on earth with its unrest, uncertainty and transience, its needs and sufferings and distress is, according to the teaching of Christ, synonymous with the "great tribulation" of which the Apocalypse speaks. *Apoc.*

Into this wicked world, dominated by the "princes of *xii. 14* this world," delivered up to darkness, and hostile to God

Jesus knew that he had been sent, not to re-organize but to save it. He was the Lamb of God, who was to take away its sins; he was the Light, that shineth in the darkness; he was the conqueror of the "princes of this world." He has brought his work to a triumphant conclusion and thus gone to the very root of suffering. The sufferings of this "aeon" will now constitute the Cross which his own must daily take up and carry along with him in the strength derived from him. As a visible and impressive proof that he was come into the world as a Redeemer he cured many sick and burdened souls, not indeed in order to free the world once for all from sickness and sorrow and want, but to bring men to a lively consciousness of the fact that one was now come who had the power to forgive sins. "Faith" as readiness and willingness to embrace the Will of God was to him of greater importance than the alleviation of sickness and suffering. Hence it was that he often demanded a profession of faith before he worked a miracle, and when he found it not he would not display his power. Nor did he work miracles for those whose faith was strong, because faith enabled men to suffer and to conquer in union with him.

The sight of the world struggling in mortal agony gave the heart of Jesus no rest until on the Cross on Golgotha he made the final sacrifice, and founded the Kingdom of the new covenant with God. But to this he was impelled more by love of God than by love of man. From the world estranged from God neither worship nor thanks nor love ascended to the throne of the Creator. It was that which caused his greatest pain and uneasiness, and which impelled him to deliver himself to the death of the Cross to implore forgiveness for the world, to make reparation and atonement and to render homage to an outraged God.

The love of Jesus for men can be estimated at its true

value only if it be considered as an overflow of his love for God. Only then does it appear truly great and worthy of him in every way. Only then does it become fully comprehensible. There is nothing in it of the lukewarm humanitarianism of a liberal age. The first place in his heart belonged to God. When the interests of the Father required it his love for mankind could take on a stern character. Never would he have allowed himself to sacrifice the interests of God to his love for mankind or his sympathy with human suffering, and it is in this that the love of Jesus shines forth in its full brilliance. It is at once beautiful, severe and ordered; it was the ruling, determining passion of his life.

Jesus faced the world calmly and earnestly. He saw it deeper and clearer than any other. The illusion of its mightiness did not terrorize him; the contemplation of its wickedness did not daunt him, nor did he despair of its ultimate salvation. Bravely and manfully he undertook the task of restoring order into the tangled web of human disorder, and this he did for all men of good will. That was a manly act of an incomparable nature, and gained for him the right to confront Mankind, through his messengers, with that final, shattering ultimatum: "He that believeth and is baptized, shall be saved; but he that believeth not shall be condemned."

Mark xvi. 16

CHAPTER V

The Man in His Struggle

I. WRESTLING WITH THE TIMES

The land of Palestine was ancient historical territory reaching back into the third century B.C. Situated as it was between the lands of the Euphrates and the Nile it was coveted by the Powers of East and West alike. Political and religious clashes were frequent there, so that down through the centuries it experienced but infrequent and short-lived periods of peace.

At the time of Christ, too, political and religious feelings ran high. Its inhabitants still remembered that in the year 63 B.C. the pagan general, Pompey, had entered the temple wearing his shoes, and thereby dishonored the all holy. Judea had been a Roman province since 6 A.D., and the yoke of slavery pressed especially heavy on a people whose boast it was that they gave allegiance to no other master than the one, true God. The pagan emperor had prescribed a tax to be paid by every adult, and this was regarded by very many as the symbol of the slavery into which they had fallen.

Revolt followed upon revolt, always with the same result. The leaders were executed and their adherents dispersed. Yet the fires of rebellion, far from being extinguished, smoldered ever under the ashes.

The people were divided. The Pharisees, on the one hand, shaped their policy that they might, at least externally, live in peace with the invader, and to this end they advised payment of the tribute. The adherents of the independent party, on the other hand, secretly instigated the people to further revolt. The Galileans were especially active in this respect, and from their hiding-places on the shores of the Lake of Genesareth they worked untiringly for the furtherance of their political aims, cloaking them under the guise of religious zeal. It was a sin, they said, to pay tribute to the Romans, and thereby acknowledge a mortal master besides God. Thus was religion used to incite political passions. Political neutrality towards the Romans was simply not tolerated, and the independents tried to win over to their side everyone of worth and authority.

In this atmosphere of hatred, unrest and suspicion the Roman soldiers and secret service agents carried out their duties. Every popular movement was suspect. The great Jewish festivals saw fresh cohorts drafted into Jerusalem for the maintenance of law and order, and pagan symbols and standards profaned the holy city to the scandal of those who still set store by the faith of their fathers.

It was likewise in this tense atmosphere, heavy with mistrust and threat of revolution, that the Man Jesus was to reveal himself as the Messias. Looked at from the merely human point of view, he was not the first to come forward with this claim. Many pretended Messiases and divine Messengers had already made their appearance within the previous decade, and such predecessors were by no means helpful to the claim of Jesus. In such environment and circumstances the mere fact that he caused a sensation and drew people to him sufficed to bring him under suspicion. The Romans suspected a new political drive; the independents secretly hoped for a new and powerful advocate of their aims, while the Pharisees feared further unrest and a consequent intensification of Roman dominion. Thus matters stood as Jesus reached the zenith of his public activity and thousands acclaimed him as a great prophet and the promised Messias. It may easily be imagined in what a dangerous position he found himself. How easily his appearance might be misinterpreted and his message misunderstood!

He had to proceed with the greatest caution if he would avoid arousing false hopes or suspicion. The slightest imprudence on his part would have sufficed to put an end to his activity and to destroy his work. His aim was neither to destroy an existing earthly kingdom nor to found a new one, but simply and solely to "give testimony of the truth," and "to seek and to save that which was lost." And his manner of acting proves how determined he was to respect existing conditions. In all his actions he was prudent but never weak, considerate but never timid; in everything he shows himself full of authority, and superiority, and he meets confidently the dangers and difficulties of any given moment. He evades or attacks as the circumstances demand, refuses to be involved in political issues, and defends himself against reproach, when it is necessary to do so. No persuasion can win him over to an unworthy cause; no threats can turn him from the right path. In everything he remains true to the spiritual Mission given him by his Father. Let us study him in some of his dealings with men.

Jesus began his public work in Judea. Already after some months a goodly number of disciples had gathered around his person. He attracted people; he was talked of. Even the Pharisees were not indifferent to him. The appearance of the Baptist had already caused them much uneasiness; they were glad and relieved when finally he was apprehended and imprisoned by Herod, perhaps not without their secret connivance. Jesus was not unaware of all this, and he had to reckon with the fact that they would soon silence him too. This he wished just then to avoid, so he eluded them and betook himself to Galilee, where he remained quietly, for he was prudent and would not unnecessarily provoke his opponents.

Quite otherwise was his behavior later on during his activity in Galilee. Here the Pharisees had noted with envy and secret fear his great success, and so they decided it was high time to withdraw him from the public eye and to push him more into the background. With this end in view they approached him in feigned friendliness to warn him of the pretended snares laid for him by Herod. "Depart and get thee hence, for Herod hath a mind to kill thee." But Jesus was not the man to be taken in by hypocritical solicitude and political threats. "Go, and tell that fox" he answered them, "Behold I cast out devils, and do cures to-day and to-morrow, and the third day I am consummated. Nevertheless, I must walk to-day and to-morrow, and the day following, because it cannot be that a prophet perish out of Jerusalem." A manly reply, which conveyed nothing less than a cool rebuff for the Pharisees, and a bold challenge to Herod! "I wander and work," so would he say to them, "where and so long as I will. When my hour is come I shall meet my death in Jerusalem in the performance of my life's task, and neither you nor Herod have the power to hinder or to hasten that hour." How like a prophetic message these words sound! What certainty, power and superiority they contain! Like a rock against which the political machinations of the Pharisees are pitiably shattered, so the Man Jesus stands before us.

Luke xiii. 31

An event related in one sentence by St. John in the sixth chapter of his Gospel emphasizes the fact that Jesus in the course of his work found himself in some very un-

pleasant situations. He was at the peak of his Galilean
activity. His reputation had penetrated to every part of
Palestine, his name was a household word. He had
preached to the multitude on the eastern bank of the
Lake of Genesareth, and afterwards in a miraculous
manner had appeased the hunger of the multitude of five
thousand men, exclusive of women and children. The
miracle had made a tremendous impression on the Gali-
John   leans. From mouth to mouth went the word: "Truly this
vi. 14   is the prophet who is to come into the world." Political
hopes and ambitions ran high once more. The Nazarene
was in their eyes the man they sought and needed: the
leader in the imminent Messianic struggle for freedom.
He possessed power over all weaknesses and illnesses. For
him there would be no problem of providing food. He
could also create weapons, as many as were needed! In
the twinkling of an eye they would have raised him
shoulder high and proclaimed him king. But quietly and
resolutely Jesus rejects their offer. With political factions
and secret societies he will have nothing to do, and
neither may he give the slightest encouragement to the
false hopes entertained by these people of earthly advancement by a Messias. And as the evangelist relates:
John   "When he knew that they would come to take him by
vi. 15   force and make him king, he fled again into the mountain himself alone."

This refusal was not without grave consequences.
Thousands withdrew from him in disappointment, and
Judas was of the number of those who rejected him,
even though outwardly he remained among his closest
followers. In his heart, however, he had transferred to
the enemy camp. But Jesus accepted calmly these defections from the ranks of his followers. He did not succumb
to popularity or become intoxicated by applause. Nor

did he fear the vengeance of the disillusioned. His way lay where the Father led.

On another occasion the Pharisees and Herodians proposed to him a very dangerous trap-question: "Is it lawful to give tribute to Caesar, or not?" It seemed that this time he was caught. If he answered in the affirmative they could denounce him to the very active agitators of the independent party, branding him as a betrayer of the religious and national heritage and thereby undermining his influence with the people. On the other hand, a negative reply would mark him as an opponent of the Roman authorities. Nothing would be easier then than to denounce him and bring about his apprehension. But Jesus suffered not a moment's embarrassment. On the contrary, he showed them clearly that he saw through their hypocrisy. "You hypocrites," he said to them, "why do you tempt me? Show me the coin of the tribute." They showed him a penny. He asked them: "Whose image and super-scription is this?" And they answered: "Caesar's." Then he said to them: "Render, therefore, to Caesar the things that are Caesar's: and to God, the things that are God's," thus conveying to them that they themselves knew perfectly well what was to be done. Why ask me? Or: Resolve these purely worldly and political questions yourselves. I will have nothing to do with them.

Matt. xxii. 15

Matt. xxii. 20

The ever-increasing difficulty of the conditions under which Jesus had to work is illustrated for us by a new development in the plan adopted by the Jewish authorities to bring about his destruction. When false depositions and religious complaints had failed to bring about the desired effect of providing adequate grounds for his death they resorted to political accusations. "We have found this man perverting our nation, and forbidding to give tribute to Caesar, and saying that he is Christ the king. . . . He stirreth up all the people, teaching throughout all Judea, beginning from Galilee to this place." The unpleasant feature of this accusation was *Luke* that it seemed to be founded on actual fact, for by his *xxiii. 2ff.* appearance and his teaching he had actually thrown the whole Jewish people into upheaval. One needs but to think of the crowds who followed him everywhere, and of that mighty sensation he had created on his entry into Jerusalem. On that occasion the whole city turned out. Who could have said whether this was a political or a religious demonstration? In any case, appearances were against him. And he would have himself proclaimed the kingly Messias! But Jesus was not in the least perturbed by these accusations. He did not experience a moment's confusion, nor lose for an instant his peace and superiority.

The impression made by his person was his most effective defense, and the clearest exposition of the real facts: "My kingdom is not of this world. If my kingdom were of this world, my servants would certainly strive that I should not be delivered to the Jews: but now my *John* kingdom is not from hence." Such a defense must at *xviii. 36* once have made clear to the Governor the real nature of the claim of Jesus, more especially since not a single soldier had appeared to support that claim. It was, therefore, obvious that he was no political leader of men.

This time the Roman's sense of justice conquered in favor of the accused. But the wily Jews soon discovered the weak point in his character, and turned it to good account. They threatened to denounce him to Caesar, and Pilate's firmness was not proof against such a threat. He delivered Jesus into the hands of the mob and spoke his death sentence.

2. ENVY, JEALOUSY, AND HATRED

Incomparable though Jesus stands among the great ones of history, he has, nevertheless, one thing in common with them: on him, too, envy, jealousy and hate worked to render his mission impossible or, should this not succeed, at least, to minimize his greatness, and to undermine his influence. We must study him in his struggle against these vigorous opponents, because the experiences he thereby made were among the bitterest of his whole life. Folly reared its head against his wisdom, envy against his achievements, jealousy against his sincerity, hatred against his kindness of heart, pettiness against his greatness, and the will to destroy against his whole person. At the Last Supper he summed up his experiences in the words: "that the word may be fulfilled which is written in their law: They hated me without cause."

John xv. 25

Who were his bitterest and most dangerous enemies? They hailed from three camps, violently opposed to one another in most other things, but one in their determination to destroy Christ: the Pharisees, the Scribes, and the Sadducees.

The Pharisees originally formed a religious lay movement, characterized by sincere goodwill, and zealous for the law in the best sense of the word. Gradually, however, their zeal deteriorated into insistence on the outward observance of the law to the exclusion of the content; the spirit was superseded by the letter. They hardened their hearts to the breath of freedom, and self love supplanted the love of God and the neighbor. They considered that they alone were just and pleasing to God, solely on the ground that they were the offspring of Abraham and familiar with the law in all its details.

The Scribes, also a lay body, busied themselves professionally with the interpretation and application of the law. They based their interpretation of the law on the "traditions of the Fathers," but gradually they substituted their own interpretation and traditions for those of the Fathers. Though they held stubbornly to traditions, they had no scruple about overstepping the actual law. Jesus found his most stubborn opponents among the Scribes.

The Sadducees, after the Pharisees the most important sect in Israel, were recruited from the priestly ranks and the wealthy patricians. As a religious body they rejected the "traditions" of the Scribes and followed strictly the wording of the law, in the interpretation of which they allowed themselves great freedom. Politically they were on the side of the Romans, and advocated generally the acceptance of Roman-Hellenistic culture and civilization. To the activity of Jesus, they at first paid very little attention, but later they joined forces with the Pharisees and Scribes in a united front against him.

The Scribes and Pharisees treated Jesus from the very outset with suspicion and distrust. The appearance of the Baptist had already caused them considerable uneasiness and indignation, but the public activity of the Nazarene fanned their wrath into flame. They dogged his footsteps. They attacked him in public and in private. They posed him trap-questions in the effort to obtain material for an accusation to the spiritual authorities. They feared his influence over the people because of the crowds which followed him everywhere. It is not to be wondered at that in the privacy of their hearts they envied and hated him. "And soon," says St. Mark, "they made a consulta-

Mark iii. 6 tion . . . against him, how they might destroy him."

The same evangelist recounts five consecutive incidents which indicate the type of reproach which the Pharisees cast at Jesus. He blasphemed God, they said, by assuming the power to forgive sins. He associated with publicans and sinners. He did not require his disciples to keep the customary fasts, and he transgressed the law of the Sabbath. He spoke against the temple and the holy Covenant, and generally despised the law and the traditions of the Fathers. They were blind to the holiness of his life, and to the power and divine freedom which emanated from him. They accounted his miracles are mere magic, or the fruit of a secret covenant with the devil. Yea, he was himself possessed of an evil spirit, and was in league with Beelzebub, the prince of devils. Such reproaches and accusations should have sufficed to make untenable his position with the common people.

There could be no more painful task for the Man Jesus, than to be compelled to announce his message of the Kingdom of God in the face of such envy, hatred and espionage. Nothing is more distressing than to discuss superior things before an audience one knows to be filled with malice and hatred. But Jesus undertook his task quietly and courageously. There is never a trace of anxiety or embarrassment, still less of that undignified fanaticism with which another might have cloaked his interior timidity. We can but admire his self-confident, upright bearing. At first he tried by a display of goodness, mildness and love to win over his opponents, or at least to bring them to an attitude of quiet, critical thought. He supported his pronouncements by miracles worked purposely in their presence: "That you may know that the Son of Man hath power on earth to forgive sins, he saith to the sick of the palsy, I say to thee, Arise, take up thy bed and go into thy house." *Mark ii. 10*

He justified his actions by reference to the Old Testament. He applied images and utterances from the prophets to his own Person in order to catch the attention of those versed in the Scriptures, and he refuted their objections so clearly that they could find no answer to his arguments, and must perforce take refuge in silence.

But all his efforts were vain. Their hearts remained obdurate; they were wanting in goodwill and drew from him the reproach: "If I had not done among them the works that no other man hath done, they would not have sin; but now they have both seen and hated both me and the Father." Gradually the rift between him and them grew wider, but he did not allow himself to be perplexed on that score. Still he warned his Apostles and the people against them: "They are blind and leaders of the blind." "Beware of the leaven of the Pharisees and Sadducees." "All things, therefore, whatsoever they shall say to you, observe and do: but according to their works do ye not: for they say, and do not. For they bind heavy and insupportable burdens: and lay them on men's shoulders, but with a finger of their own they will not move them." Finally he publicly exposed them before the whole people when he spoke his threat of "Woe to you, Scribes and Pharisees." It was his final reckoning with them, and perhaps the most terrible that any man had ever made in public with his opponents. Even now as we read the twenty-third chapter of St. Matthew's Gospel we can almost see his lips tremble and hear his voice quiver with emotion and holy wrath as he utters the fateful words. Like an apocalyptic judgement his words smite their ears. And he must have been quite clear as to the consequences for himself. But he was prepared to drain the cup of their vengeance to the very dregs, and he knew that they had already planned his death.

In this struggle with the Scribes and Pharisees Jesus manifested all the riches of his manly nature. By turns he coaxed and threatened, invited and rejected, treated them with indulgence or lashed them with his anger; he

John xv. 24

Matt. xv. 14 xvi. 16 xxiii. 3

bore them with patience, but hesitated not, when occasion demanded, to tear the mask from their countenances. But in all he mirrored perfect strength, self-confidence and self-control. Those who heard his words and watched his behavior were constrained to agree with him. His opponents were morally annihilated even before they struck him the final blow. Like dwarfs they cowered before this giant, like pitiful nonentities before this unconquerable Strong One.

As in the struggle with his opponents so did Jesus stand the test before his judges. Each new trial, each new tribunal showed him in the light of a new greatness. The high priest wanted to interrogate him concerning his disciples and his teaching. But Jesus answered him: "I have spoken openly to the world: I have always taught in the synagogue, and in the temple whither all the Jews resort; and in secret I have spoken nothing. Why asketh thou me? Ask them who have heard what I have spoken unto them: behold they know what things I have said." A magnificently daring rebuff to a man who had, indeed, no right whatever to bring Jesus to trial. And one which earned him a blow from one of the servants standing by as he said: "Answerest thou the high-priest so?" But for him too the accused had a suitable retort: "If I have spoken evil, give testimony of the evil; but if well, why strikest thou me?" What courage, what upright, manly bearing in such an hour! *John xviii. 19ff.*

Before Caiphas and the supreme council he answered the false and contradictory accusations made against him with studied silence, thus compelling the crafty Sanhedrin to give the correct replies. But to the final official question: "Art thou the Messias, the Son of the Blessed God?" he made a clear, frank avowal, although well aware that it was a matter of life and death, "I am." And to the great consternation of his judges, he imme- *Matt. xxvi. 57ff.* *Mark xvi. 61, 62* diately follows up this acknowledgment of his divinity with a flight into the supernatural: "Amen, I say to you, you shall see the Son of Man sitting on the right hand of the power of God, and coming with the clouds of heaven." The tables were turned; the accused became the threatening judge of those who sat in judgment upon him.

Luke xxiii. 8ff.

Herod considered him a magician and a charlatan, and would gladly have rewarded him with his princely favor if the accused had been willing to gratify him and his court by a display of magic power. But the Man Jesus knew how to keep his dignity, and by his complete silence he caused Herod such embarrassment that the latter could find no means of escape from the awkwardness of the situation except in treating Jesus as a fool.

Before Pilate Jesus used alternately a studied speech and silence like an admonishing conscience so that the Governor was compelled again and again to affirm the innocence of the accused, even while, through cowardice, he uttered the death sentence.

On the Cross he brought about the conversion of the thief by his sufferings borne with manly and superhuman courage and patience, and drew from the lips of the centurion the confession: "Indeed this man was the Son of God."

Mark xv. 39

Thus Jesus remained victor in the struggle against envy, jealousy and hatred, despite the seeming destruction which the heavenly Father allowed to befall him. That which God spoke to the prophet Jeremias, that manly forerunner, and companion in misfortune of the Man of Nazareth, when he called him to his mission, was even more wonderfully fulfilled in the life and destiny of the Man Jesus: "I have made thee this day a fortified city and a pillar of iron and a wall of brass over all the land, to the Kings of Juda, to the princes thereof,

and to the priests and to the people of the land. And they
shall fight against thee and shall not prevail, for I am
with thee to deliver thee."

Jer.
i. 18f.

Nay, even though they nailed him to the Cross they
did not prevail.

3. HIS LONELINESS

If we would in some measure appreciate the heroic
struggle which the man Jesus waged against the obstacles
he met with in carrying out of his mission we must
try to enter into the infinite loneliness in which he lived
his life. We may in a small way be helped to this realization if we consider his loneliness under a double aspect,
the divine and human. Naturally we must hasten to add
that in actual fact there is question only of one infinite
loneliness. As the Son of God Jesus walked the earth
among men in an indescribable, incomprehensible loneliness. Even as he could, in an altogether unique way,
call God Father, and must speak of "his" Father, exclusive of the Apostles, so must we speak of "his" loneliness. Not a single soul of those who shared his daily life
was able to understand him, not a single one could participate in his plans and in his work. "No one knoweth
the Son but the Father . . . and he to whom it shall
please the Son to reveal Him." Only those, therefore,
could know him whom he himself called, to whom he
revealed himself, and in whose hearts he himself im-
planted his grace, his truth and his love. This, his divine
loneliness, there was no possibility of dissipating, or even
relieving, by any mere earthly or human means. The
only access to this loneliness was from above, whence
indeed could come its complete alleviation, as he himself
indicated with the words: "The hour cometh, and it is
now come, that you shall be scattered every man to his

Matt.
xi. 27

own, and shall leave me alone; and yet I am not alone, *John* because the Father is with me."
xvi. 32

But the years of his public activity for the Man Jesus were years of an unspeakable human loneliness. It need not necessarily have been so. He might have looked to his fellow-creatures for at least a partial lightening and alleviation of his burden. One can readily imagine that there were around him persons endowed with geniality and greatness of character who would willingly have provided him with companionship, who would have comforted him with a deep and lively understanding, and whom he would not repeatedly have to reproach: "O, foolish, and slow of heart to believe." "Are you also *Luke* yet without understanding?" "Do you not yet under-
xxiv. 25 stand?" and of whom the evangelist would not be com-
Matt. pelled to relate: "Then the disciples all leaving him,
xv. 16
xvi. 9 fled." But such was not the Will of Him who would
Matt. "deliver up" his Son for men, and who sent him to call
xxvi. 56 the little ones and the lowly that he might manifest to us a new greatness.

In the accomplishment of his task the Man Jesus found in his immediate environment neither support nor help from any quarter. We see him abandoned at the most decisive junctures. And even if his disciples could not understand all that he planned and spoke—many things they could not yet bear, so Jesus said—yet he might have expected from them a more lively spirit of faith and a keener apprehension of the things he spoke and did, a more co-operative spirit, a more selfless, sympathetic companionship. But instead we perceive among their number repeated trivial squabblings for position, lack of self-control, fear and anxiety and a mass of prejudices. Let us take a few examples for our consideration.

They had been frequently enough witnesses of the

hypocrisy, duplicity, wickedness and suspicious character of the Pharisees, whom Jesus had often contradicted and reduced to silence in their presence. Now he once more warns the Apostles against them: "take heed and beware of the leaven of the Pharisees and Sadducees." One would have thought they could have deduced his meaning from this metaphor, but the Gospel narrative shows clearly that they took his words literally and wrestled with their meaning: "they thought within themselves," the evangelist says, and finally came to the conclusion that he meant "we have taken no bread."

Matt. xvi. 6f.

For three long years he had labored to correct their false representations of the Messias. And yet after his Resurrection on the way to Mount Olivet, in spite of his having deliberately unveiled to them the secrets of the kingdom of God, they blurted out the question: "Lord, wilt thou at this time restore again the kingdom to Israel?" Many other like examples of their short-sightedness are recorded for us in the Gospel pages.

Acts i. 6

In his heavy, momentous discussion with the Scribes and Pharisees—for these, too, were of the number of those he had come to seek and to save—the Apostles afforded him neither support nor encouragement. He could not turn to them for advice. He was always compelled to shoulder the responsibility alone, though he must frequently have been confronted with the problem whether it was wiser to meet his opponents with mildness or severity, with silence or reprimand. On the contrary, the Apostles too hampered him in his struggle. For they fell a prey to anxiety and timidity and would warn and restrain him, and to them also he had to give encouragement and spiritual support, "Fear ye not them that kill the body, and are not able to kill the soul." Thus he comforted them in their despondency. When consequent on the multiplication of the loaves and fishes he had

Matt. x. 28

refused his consent to be made King, and had delivered
in Capharnaum his great discourse on the Blessed
Eucharist, and spoken of the eating of his flesh and the
drinking of his blood, we read that many of his followers
left him. They murmured against him and said: "This

John saying is hard, and who can hear it." Even his Apostles
vi. 61ff. stood by, dazed, helpless and bewildered. But Jesus boldly
ran the risk of this final isolation and himself formulated
for his Apostles the decisive question: "Will you also go
away?" Let us try to picture to ourselves the tremendous
tension of this moment! He was determined to accept
this complete isolation of his person, but the doctrine
which he had formulated he would not soften or rescind
by so much as a word. What strength of soul, what
courage, what character were needed to face up to such
a stupendous issue! But Jesus faced up to it.

In what abysmal loneliness Jesus uttered the prophecies
concerning his Passion! For it was his own person that
was immediately concerned when he announced to his
Apostles: "Behold we go up to Jerusalem, and all things
shall be accomplished which were written by the
Prophets concerning the Son of Man. For he shall be
delivered to the Gentiles and shall be mocked, and

Luke scourged, and spit upon." He might have expected
xvii. 31–34 them, at least by a question, to express their interest and
sympathy, or in some way to manifest their willingness
to accompany him. Peter did, indeed, make a half-
hearted attempt to distract the Master from his troubled
thoughts. He drew him aside, and said to him earnestly:

Matt. "Lord, be it far from thee, this shall not be unto thee."
xvi. 22 But this outburst was prompted more by personal fear
and self-protection than by real sympathy with his
Master. And it denoted a mentality far removed from
the designs of Jesus and that which the Will of God had
ordained, and therefore, it won for Peter a sharp rebuke.

"Go behind me, satan, thou art a scandal unto me, because thou savorest not the things that are of God, but the things that are of man." Thus it was with all his predictions of his sufferings: "They understood none of these things, and this word was hid from them." Finally they dared not question him any further concerning his Passion. On their way to Jerusalem, as Jesus boldly and determinedly preceded them "they were astonished, and following were afraid." Consider the loneliness of this man. *Luke xviii. 34*

Luke xviii. 34

This loneliness reached its climax in the supper room where Jesus was present for the last time with his Apostles. From the cordial, almost appealing tone of his final discourse to them we can deduce how infinitely lonely he felt in the circle of his friends during these last hours before his Passion. The conversation and questions of his Apostles show that they were utterly indifferent to the sadness which sat upon his countenance, and quite unaware of the momentousness of the occasion and of what was taking place. They convey an impression of peculiar helplessness, one might say of immaturity. They do not in any sense stand by him, and they seem to be altogether indifferent to his thoughts and mode of acting, so that we are not in the least surprised that they are completely bewildered by the tragic events which follow. In the Garden while the Master wrestles with the agony of his soul, and can scarcely formulate a few dry words of prayer because of the burden of sorrow, anxiety and desolation which bears down on him, they fall dead asleep, and when his abysmal loneliness impels him to utter a gentle reproach: "Could you not watch one hour with me?" they scarcely hear him, "their eyes were heavy, and they knew not what to answer him." *Matt. xxvi. 40*

It was night. Jerusalem slept, and the whole world slept the sleep of sin and indifference. There was only *Matt. xiv. 37* one who watched, only one who could save the world, and he only by unspeakable sufferings, loneliness, and humiliation. That one was Jesus. On him it depended whether the great work would be accomplished or not. He needed not the world or men. No internal or external compulsion obliged him to undergo the horror of the Passion. But with manly fortitude he accepted and drained the chalice of suffering which the Father held to his lips, he alone!

His interior suffering was increased a thousandfold by the knowledge that one of the little company of twelve had delivered him over to the enemy with the traitor's kiss, that another of them had thrice denied him, and that, one and all, they had abandoned him in the hour of his greatest need. And so his loneliness gradually gathered impetus until on the Cross it was given him to taste of that final, mysterious desolation when the Father Himself veiled His countenance, and the lips of the dying Savior were constrained to give utterance to the abandonment of his soul in that last agonized cry: "My God, my God, why hast Thou forsaken me!"

Isaias
lxiii. 3   "I have trodden the wine-press alone and of the Gentiles there is not a man with me." In these words the prophet Isaias had fortetold the loneliness of the Man of Nazareth.

CHAPTER VI

The God-Man

I. GOD'S IMAGE AND LIKENESS

As the Roman centurion stood beneath the cross on Golgotha and witnessed all that took place at the death of Christ he gave utterance to the cry: "Indeed, this man was the Son of God." The pagan could hardly have understood in the Christian sense the Divine Sonship which he attributed to Christ. He may have sensed in him the self-revelation of a divinity, or held him for an unknown demi-god, but whatever other thoughts exercised his mind in relation to Christ, *one* thing was supreme: this was no ordinary man. Such patience and fortitude under the most appalling of death struggles, such distinction of bearing and magnanimity even towards his enemies, no mere ordinary man would be capable of. An unknown deity, or, at least, divine strength must here have manifested itself in human shape. Legend has it that the centurion later became a Christian and sealed his faith with his blood, but whether or not this be true, the import of the story is obviously true, that the superhuman heroism of the Man Jesus paved the way for the unprejudiced onlooker to faith in his real Godhead. We can the more readily grasp this intellectual process if we consider that his manly great-

Mark xv. 35

125

ness, as indeed his whole manhood, bears a particular relationship to the divine. There is a reference to this in the eleventh chapter of the first epistle to the Corinthians, in which St. Paul lays down instructions for the behavior of men and women at divine worship. *Inter alia,* he states that men should assist at divine worship with uncovered heads, while women, on the contrary, should have their heads covered, and for our purpose the reasons which lead him to this decision are important.

I Cor. "The man indeed ought not to cover his head, because
xi. 7ff. he is the image and glory of God; but the woman is the glory of the man. For the man is not of the woman, but the woman of the man. For the man was not created for the woman, but the woman for the man. . . . But I
ii. 3ff. would have you know, that the head of every man is Christ: and the head of the woman is the man: and the head of Christ is God. Every man praying or prophesying with his head covered, disgraceth his head."

In these words the Apostle furnishes us with a symbol of manhood. Man is "the image and likeness of God." This characterization may strike us as insignificant or inconsistent in the light of the account in Genesis where the woman is described equally with the man as the
Gen. image of God. How then can Paul call man, in distinc-
i. 26ff. tion to woman, the image and likeness of God? For either his words convey nothing of a differentiating nature of the man as opposed to the woman, or they are in direct contradiction to the account in Genesis.

Let us first of all ask ourselves in what exactly consists the superiority, the distinction which accrues to man from this characterization as the image and likeness of God. It must immediately be noted that the notion of man as the likeness of God is surprisingly rare in the whole of the Old Testament; it occurs only a few times expressly or by insinuation. In general the faith of the

Old Testament is grounded fundamentally on the principle of man's infinite distance from God; man appears before God as dust and ashes, "as the grass on the housetops, that withereth ere it is plucked up." Were he to presume to approach too near to the All-high he would be consumed by the fire of the Divine Sanctity and Majesty. In view of such assertions the characteristic of likeness to God remained almost altogether in the background, and only incidentally, as it were, is man referred to as God's image. And yet there is no doubt about it, that this constitutes the finest and noblest and most astounding thing about man; it is just this that gives the Old Testament pronouncements on man their superiority over those of the pagan myths and religions, for in the Old Testament man appears plunged in the secret springs of the Divine Essence.

Isaias xxxvii. 27

If then we consider these statements as a whole there emerges the fact that by the likeness of man to God it is not intended to indicate a purely spiritual quality, nor possibly only the spiritual, immortal soul, but something which concerns the whole human being, something visible which the ordinary man can observe, establish and verify for himself. It becomes accordingly a question of something sensible, something imposing and striking in the human being as opposed to other living creatures, and therefore it may be asserted that the grandeur of man's external apearance is an expression of the image and likeness of God to which he is made, and this is even more true of the interior spiritual wealth and power, superiority and dignity which are his as a free personality. He stands, as it were the living embodiment of God's power in the world, the representative of his sovereign rights, and as a spirit-informed, free, personal being he is the visible expression of the dominion of God in so far as he exists in himself and rules the whole world in sovereign majesty. In this consists the peculiar superiority and dignity of the human being, in this are man and woman equal, in this are both alike distinguished, and because of this they stand apart among all other living beings.

What, then, does St. Paul mean to convey when he calls man alone the "image and likeness of God" and woman merely "the image of man?" He may have had in mind the actual process of creation when God first and directly created man and then woman from the side of the man, thus placing man in a certain direct relationship to God, whereas the reflection of God reached woman, as it were, indirectly through man. The Apostle himself justifies his assertions concerning man and woman in the words: "The man is not of the woman, but the woman of the man; for the man was not created for the woman, but the woman for the man."

But there is a deeper meaning to be sought in the words of the Apostle. The notion of the "image and likeness of God" has a further extension in the relation of the sexes to one another. The man with his creative talents and predisposition to activity, as worker and weaver, images the mighty creative, governing activity of the omnipotent God, while the woman with her capacity for surrender, for the reception and development of the life begotten of the man is an image of creation. So the human being is a reflection of God, living and resting in himself, and sovereignly governing the universe, the man of the creator, the woman of creation.

This idea of man and mankind as the image of God requires further consideration, since it throws a particular light on the figure of the Man Jesus, who occupies a unique position in the world of men, and has proved himself in the truest and most sublime sense the image and likeness of the Creator. By him was the work of Redemption perfected; from him, the founder of the kingdom of God, originates the "new creation" the "new Man."

II Cor. v. 17

He is the bridegroom of the Church, who "loved it, and delivered himself up for it, that he might sanctify it, cleansing it by the laver of water in the word of life, that he might present it to himself a glorious Church, not having spot or wrinkle, or any such thing, but that it should be holy and without blemish." Thus in his creative activity he proved himself the image and likeness of God.

Eph. v. 25ff.

And none had ever undertaken and accomplished so mighty a work as he, never was human life devoted so unequivocally and exclusively to a work as his was, never did man contribute such stirring events to history. He was creator, leader, savior, redeemer—in a word, complete and perfect man, as St. Paul says "head of man," the spiritual origin and permanent prototype of all mankind, so that all manly worth is but the image and participation of his dignity. The first man, Adam, was but a "figure of him who was to come," the "second" better Adam, the "one man Jesus Christ." Only in him was perfectly fulfilled the creative thought contained in the solemn pronouncement: "Let us make man to our own image and likeness."

Rom. v. 14 I Cor. xv. 45

Did this characteristic of the divine image in any way reveal itself in the external appearance of Christ? No portrait of Christ has come down to us to inform us on this point. In the Old Testament portraiture was prohibited by law. The Jews might not represent to themselves pictorially the invisible, spiritual Deity, and they loyally observed this prohibition. In their anxiety to prevent abuses they even prevented human beings from being thus represented. "All pictures are permitted, except those of human beings," ran an old law. This attitude was determined by the likeness to God attributed to the human being, for a human likeness might very easily be set up as that of God, and this their reverence for God would never allow. And so it is quite intelligible that the early Christians, too, should have neglected to leave to posterity a portrait of Christ.

Nevertheless, by an extraordinary dispensation of Divine Providence we have been presented with a true and authentic reproduction of the figure and person of Jesus, not prepared by any human hand.

From the Gospel accounts we learn that the dead body of Jesus, a short time after his death, was removed from the cross by Joseph of Arimathea, and wrapped in fine linen. Quite unclothed, his sacred body was laid on one half of the sheet and covered over with the other half. By means of physical, chemical processes liberated by the still fever-racked body, covered with blood and wounds a negative picture of the Crucified became phototechnically imprinted on this winding-sheet, which is still preserved, as the most treasured possession of the Italian Royal Family, in the Chapel of the Holy Shroud in Turin, and which furnishes us with a reliable picture, not only of the countenance, but of the whole figure of Jesus from back and front. The countenance of Christ, as it has been given to us in this apparently fortuitous, but really providential manner, affects one profoundly. It is the countenance of a dead man, but of one who obviously had power over death, so much life still flows from those calm features. It is the countenance of a Crucified who but recently had been convulsed by the pangs of unimaginable suffering—the marks of the crown of thorns are clearly visible on the brow; the jaw is disfigured by the blows he had been dealt, the nose broken. But despite all this the face radiates a calm and majesty, a simplicity and dignity which has defied reproduction by all the artistic talent and piety of even the greatest masters. Even had it not already been scientifically established that this portrait of Christ was not drawn by any human hand, it would yet be obvious from the arresting impression made by it that it is more than a human masterpiece.

But the Holy Shroud of Turin reveals not merely the nobility and perfection of the countenance of Christ; it gives us also valuable information regarding the external appearance of the whole body. We find thereon confirmed what the evangelical accounts suggest, that Jesus was an imposing figure, nearly six feet tall, powerfully built, harmonious and symmetrical, man and Master from the crown of his head to the soles of his feet. How could it have been otherwise with the Son of the pure and tender virgin, of whom the Canticle sings: "Thou art all fair, my beloved." How could this soul, generated by Divine Strength and Beauty, have taken to itself a body less than perfect! For in him the most beautiful of the sons of men walked this earth.

Perhaps it was well that no human hand dared to depict the living features of the Man Christ, for even the most gifted artist could have left us only his personal impression of the figure of Jesus, and who could hope to portray in any measure the fullness of the interior life and the soul which shone through this exterior form!

Not in vain did the Holy Spirit prompt four men to write the Gospel of Jesus Christ. They left behind four spiritual Christ-pictures which, by complementing and completing one another, become fused into one single portrait. That which is expressed in this single portrait of noblest humanity, sovereignty and mastery, of goodness and mildness, strength and ardor, mystery and sanctity, stamps the possessor of all these attributes and qualities as par excellence the very image and likeness of

God. Thus appeared the infinite God when He deigned to permit His glory to shine forth among men under human form.

There is yet a further sense in which Christ in the scriptures is called the image of God. In the Second Epistle to the Corinthians we read: "The God of this world hath blinded the minds of unbelievers, that the light of the Gospel of the Glory of Christ, who is the image of God should not shine unto them." In the first chapter of the Epistle to the Colossians Paul speaks of Christ "who is the image of the invisible God, the first-born of every creature." And in the introduction to the epistle to the Hebrews we find him referred to as "the brightness of his (God's) glory and the figure of his substance." In these words the inspired writer applies to Christ what is expressed of Divine Wisdom in the seventh chapter of the Book of Wisdom: "She is the brightness of eternal light . . . and the image of his goodness."

II Cor. iv. 4

Col. i. 15

The expression "image" in the New Testament generally signifies, not merely the reflected image, but the actual, original figure visibly expressed in its essence. When, therefore, Christ is referred to as the "image," "Brightness," "figure and likeness" of God and the Divine Essence it is intended to express that he is the origin, that is, God Himself, co-equal with Him. It is simply an expression of the Divinity. To be the image of God simply means to be in the form of God. Thus the image of God as applied to Christ is merely an attempt to express his Sonship in another way. And his Divinity is likewise expressed in the words he himself spoke to Philip in the supper-room: "He that seeth me, seeth the Father also."

John xiv. 9

In a threefold splendor then, does the image of God shine through the figure of Jesus: as man he is the image and likeness of the Creator; as human being, the image and likeness of God as He exists in Himself; as Son of God, the "brightness of the glory and figure of the substance" of God, co-equal with the Father and dwelling with Him in the unity of a single Godhead. Image here meets image, likeness becomes one with likeness and splendor merges into splendor. It is only when we observe the Man of Nazareth in this threefold splendor that we can, in any measure, touch the fullness which has here below corporeally appeared in him.

Jesus was man. But he was more than man; he was Son of God. The limitations of his humanity become merged in the Divine, but even there where they lose themselves completely in the mysterious depths of the Divinity they still preserve their original human lines, for it is always one and the same splendor which lights up the figure of Jesus: that of the image and likeness of God.

2. THE WAY, THE TRUTH, AND THE LIFE

It is a generally accepted fact that men have played a far greater role in history than women. The intellectual life of peoples, the development of their culture, and their progress in science and technique have been, for the most part, man's achievement. This is not the result of mere blind chance, or sociological misproportion, more or less implying that woman in the earlier centuries was considered inferior to man and debarred from intellectual advancement.

The reason lies deeper, and is to be sought rather in the physical-intellectual structure of the two sexes. By inclination and natural tendency the man is more fitted for creative work than the woman. He is the born originator, shaper and enterpriser. His intellect enables him with comparative facility to select from a diversity of things and conditions the most important, the governing, the decisive elements. His will concerns itself with the object rather than with the person. He is a fighter and conqueror, he finds his pleasure in building and shaping, in leading and inspiring, and in the awakening of physical and mental life.

Within this psychological premise let us turn once again to the character of Jesus. At the last supper he said *John xiv. 1ff.* to his Apostles: "Let not your heart be troubled. You believe in God, believe also in me. In my father's house there are many mansions. If not, I would have told you, because I go to prepare a place for you: I will come again, and will take you to myself, that where I am, you also may be. And whither I go you know, and the way you know! Thomas saith to him: Lord, we know not whither thou goest, and how can we know the way. Jesus saith to him: I am the Way, and the Truth and the Life. No man cometh to the Father, but by me. If you had known me, you would without doubt have known my Father also; and from henceforth you shall know him, and you have seen him."

John xiv. 6 Jesus makes this pronouncement out of the inexpressible depths of his self-knowledge. "I am the way and the truth and the life." We might interpret this assertion as the self-confession of a man, happy in the fulfillment of his manhood, who knew the mission of man, and was ready to devote himself and all his powers to the accomplishment of his task. He was a pioneer, a preacher of the truth, an awakener of life as none other had been. He alone had beaten a path whose luminous track led men to the feet of God. None other had proclaimed such clear, decisive truths. Hence it does not suffice to think of him as the greatest figure in human history; he had no parallel, he was unique among men; in him manhood found its fullest and richest and most marvellous development.

But these assertions do not touch the essential factor in his being. While we consider him merely as the greatest among the giants of history we are not doing justice to his claim. He did not come "from below" so that he might be raised to the highest; he came "from above." His appearance stands for something fundamentally new and hitherto unheard of in the world of men, a unique and peculiar gift from on high. His way begins with God and leads through the world to lose itself once more in God. His truth reveals God, illumines minds and links them up with God. His life takes its source from God, renews mankind and flows back again to God. This identity with the Godhead is the greatest mystery in this man's character.

But even with this we have not plumbed the last and ultimate depths of his personality. What has been said of him thus far is true of every saint and prophet. His self-revelation embraces much more. For here is a man who does not merely indicate a way; he is the way itself: he is not only a revealer of the truth, but the truth itself, not an awakener of life, but life itself. And with this revelation he places himself unequivocally on the level of the Godhead. The splendor of his manhood penetrates into the depths of his divinity, but even as it grows dim in the distance its gentle glow throws into relief the manly features of the God-man. Let us follow the traces of this transition.

The Way

I am the way. No human being before or since Christ had dared to give expression to such a statement. There have been no lack of persons who would point out new methodical ways to God. Some there were who would send men on the road of contemplation and self-abnegation; others have tried to find the way to God through pious activity and the observance of rites, laws and regulations; still others have trodden the path of asceticism and subjugated the body in order to liberate the spirit for the ascent to God. But the Man Jesus taught no way, preached no method by which man could, so to speak, press on with mechanical inevitability to the possession of God. He presented himself as the living, personal way, avowing of himself: "No man cometh to the *John xiv. 6* Father, but by me." He was and is, the one and only *I Tim.* "Mediator between God and man." All religious media- *ii. 5* tion which at any time has been ascribed to kings and priests and prophets has found its fulfillment in him. Mankind had wandered from the right path. "All we like sheep have gone astray, everyone hath turned aside *Is.* into his own way." Ever since the founder of the human *viii. 6* race had trodden the way of sin our relationship with God was awry, and the way to God and to our own salvation was obstructed. Then came the man Jesus to sponsor the cause of erring mankind. He negotiated the great reconciliation by offering to God reparation and *Hebrews* satisfaction through the surrender of his Body and Blood *ix. 15* for us. Thus he became "the Mediator of the New Testa- *x. 9ff.* ment," giving us "a confidence in the entering into the Holies by the Blood of Christ, a new and living way which he hath dedicated for us through the veil, that is to say, his flesh." This was the sublime task he set himself. He wished to be the way for mankind lost in darkness, the patient servant of God who gave his life as a sin-offering, the open door for the scattered sheep, the courageous shepherd who risked his life for the wandering ones of his flock. In all that he showed himself a man, though in a way which infinitely surpassed all that any other living man could possibly achieve.

By revealing himself as a superhumanly influential

leader and guide of the destiny of mankind Jesus unfolded his manhood.

He pointed to himself as the way of salvation not only for Israel, but for the whole world. On its attitude to his person depends the eternal destiny of the human race, and therefore he demanded a complete surrender to his person and leadership. It did not suffice to say "Lord, Lord;" he required to be followed and imitated. "He that loveth father or mother more than me is not worthy of me." "No man putteth his hand to the plough, and looking back, is fit for the Kingdom of God." "He that taketh not up his cross, and followeth me, is not worthy of me."

Matt. x. 37
Luke ix. 62
Matt. x. 38

He assumes to himself supreme authority as the greatest and most binding law-giver. From the lips of the Old Testament prophets there frequently falls the phrase: "Thus saith the Lord." But from Jesus we never hear such words. He speaks in his own name. On his own initiative he revises and corrects the old laws. His activity is, indeed, that of a prophet, but he takes his stand there whence all other prophets have been sent, on the level of the Godhead.

His person is the measure of all justice. He demands that we accomplish the highest moral tasks for his sake. For his sake we are called on to suffer hatred and persecution; for his sake must we immolate and conquer ourselves, renounce worldly goods, even forego the love of his creatures. A good deed done in his name, no matter how insignificant in itself, means something great before God, and on Judgment Day will receive its reward.

Not only decisive claims and glittering promises, but likewise final threats come from his person. These concern in the first place the city of Jerusalem which has not known the hour of its visitation by him, the Messias. But they apply equally to all whose attitude is similar to that of the unrepentent city. He is the corner-stone over which the obdurate of heart stumble to their destruction; he is the master of the house who closes his doors to those whom he cannot acknowledge as his own.

In everything which concerns the destiny of mankind he has a very definite role to play. Where there is a way that leads to, and loses itself in God, it is of his making. When after laborious wanderings a soul ultimately reaches its goal, it is to find to its great surprise that it was all the time on the road to him. He is at once the guide and the leader, the way and the goal. Nobody comes to the Father except by him.

The Truth

In the course of the centuries many have appeared with the claim that they had important and decisive truths to impart to mankind, but none has ever dared to present himself to men as the personification of the truth. He would have been branded as insane if he made such a claim. But Jesus called himself the Truth, and so self-evident does the claim sound from his lips and so much in keeping with the total impression of his being, that there is a risk that we shall overlook the significance of this unusual utterance.

What did Jesus wish to convey by this avowal? It is not possible, nor is it our purpose, to give here an exhaustive exposition of the meaning of the term "aletheia" used by Jesus, but it is up to us to let the virile quality of this avowal sink well into our hearts. The Man Jesus pronounced the words: "I am the Truth." We shall endeavor, in some small measure, to discover the significance of these simple words.

The word "aletheia" as it is used in the New Testament is characterized by a strong, virile, ringing sound. It signifies firm or fixed, something that possesses validity or durability, something that man can rely on, hence reliability, loyalty, uprightness, honesty. Furthermore, it implies the actual in contrast to the seeming, the truth in contrast to untruth, the true faith in contrast to false doctrine.

All these significations are somehow expressed in the self-revelation contained in the words: "I am the Truth." The Man Jesus is the personification of all that is lasting, genuine, reliable and sound. Everything about him is open and upright; in his attitude there is nothing that is artificial or puffed up or obtrusive. The Apocalypse describes him as the "Faithful and True."

Apoc.
xix. 11

Truth in the sense of a sane, honest outlook speaks above all from the spiritual life of the Man Jesus. His is an unequalled, superhuman perfection. He combines the greatest clarity of thought with absolute certainty of judgment. He is never embarrassed, never compelled to revise or withdraw his words. He never hesitates about a decision, and his knowledge embraces past, present and future.

To him we are indebted, above all, for a new portrait of the Divinity. In this matter, also, mankind had strayed from the path of truth, and produced images of the Deity which were mere caricatures. Men were regarded as the playthings of the gods, who mocked at their burdens. But with sure touch the Man Jesus frees the image of God from all such unworthy misrepresentation, and it is only since his advent we really understand the meaning of religion and piety. He has furnished us with the most sublime revelation of the Father. His wisdom penetrates into the most mysterious depths of the Divine Origin, and none but he can gaze with uncovered eye into the sun of the Divine Effulgence. He alone can speak of the most sublime mysteries of the Godhead with the loving familiarity of a child relating the splendors of his paternal home, as he alone can interpret the most hidden Divine thoughts with the certainty of one who speaks of his personal experiences.

All this Jesus wished to convey to men when he avowed himself the Truth. He would thereby set himself up as the Divine Reality and Reliability in contrast to the capricious, unreliable nature of man, as the personal Revelation of the Divine Efficacy. For he is not, as the prophets, merely the mouthpiece of God; everything he does and says is God's direct revelation. He is the Word of God. He is himself God. Therefore he is the Truth.

Therefore this revelation rings clear as a trumpet-call, and full "as the sound of many waters." The super-humanly great and mysterious God-man speaks to us.

Apoc. i. 15

The Life

When Holy Scripture speaks of life in the religious sense, there is not meant the natural life of man which ends in death. Life is understood in a higher sense and includes indestructibility. Real, true, perfect life knows not death. It is eternal, as God is eternal. Hence he is called the Living. To Him belongs original, indestructible life. In contrast with that life our natural life here on earth is something provisional, and men may, although in possession of this life, be said to be dead. This true, higher life, often referred to in Scripture simply as "the life" man does not bring with him into this world. It must be given him by God as a gift of grace.

Religious salvation consists in the possession by man of this life. He must acquire it by corresponding moral behavior, and in this sense he may go "the way of life" or "the way of death." He is not able of himself alone to gain this life or to ensure its future possession. God must awaken him to life and preserve him in it. That He is willing and ready to do so—on that is founded Christian faith and hope.

This awakening took place primarily and perfectly in Jesus Christ. Him, the human being, did God raise from death to life, not again to life in a mortal body but in a glorified body. That was the reward for his suffering and death for the redemption of mankind. And in virtue of his redemptive act the gift of resurrection will be granted to us also. He has become, not only "the first-born from the dead" but also "the Author of Life." Our eternal *Col. i. 18* salvation consists in that we shall become participators *Acts iii. 15* in his life. He is our life. In him it exists in divine abundance, and from him as the source and fountain-head it flows down into the members of his body.

Once again, then, he stands before us in superhuman greatness as he avows of himself: "I am the Life." By this he does not mean the natural, cosmic life which all living creatures possess, but that higher supernatural life in which our salvation consists. This life which you seek and need, but which you cannot give yourselves—thus would he give his Apostles to understand—that exists in me in great abundance. I am the author of life, because I am life itself, as God is life. Everything that I do among you on earth is a revelation and a communication of that life, because I am the Son of God become man. "For as the Father hath life in himself; so he hath given to the Son also to have life in himself." *John*
v. 26

To become the author of life, whether in a physical or in a spiritual sense, is the task of man. The stronger this life pulses in the veins of his descendants the more the manhood of the author is manifested and glorified. The Man Jesus by his work of redemption "destroyed death, and hath brought to light life and incorruption." He has *II Tim.* become the author of the only immortal life. The infinite *i. 10* vitality of God dwelt originally in him; he *was* this vitality in Divine Person, and so once more the glory of his manhood is reflected from the depths of his Godhead.

3. THE SON OF MAN

As we have already seen, Jesus avoided any direct and obtrusive reference to himself as the Messias. This reticent attitude was necessary because of the false Messianic images and hopes current among the Jews, and with which he dared not identify himself. Hence he cloaked his Messianic avowals under the title "Son of Man." This name was sufficient to convey to his hearers his sublime mission, while not being one of the recognized Messianic titles in use among the Jews.

The title "Son of Man" was not primarily intended to give expression to the power and strength of him who bore it; on the contrary, it indicated membership of the weak, vacillating human race, and it is in this sense it is generally used in the Old Testament. It is significant of the masculine self-consciousness of Jesus that he forebore to apply the expression, "Son of Man," in this sense to his person. He used it rather in the sense of a strong, vigorous man, as it is used only once in the Old Testament, where we read in the seventh chapter of the Book of Daniel: "I beheld in the vision of the night, and lo, one like the Son of Man came with the clouds of Heaven. And he came even to the Ancient of days, and they presented him before him. And he gave him power and *Daniel* glory and a kingdom, and all peoples, tribes and tongues *vii. 13f.* shall serve him. His power is an everlasting power that shall not be taken away, and his kingdom that shall not be destroyed." This powerful king, whose dominion surpassed the bounds of time and space, Jesus would identify himself with. As such he knew himself, and therefore, he did not call himself merely *a* Son of Man, but *The* Son of Man.

All Jesus' preaching centered around the thought of the Last Judgment. He supported his call to penance with a warning of the severe judgment that awaited every man. He repeatedly comes back to this theme, but his is not only the role of preacher, he also claims to be the judge in this judgment. For the Son of Man of Daniel's vision who came in the clouds of heaven is none other than the Divine Judge himself. What gigantic stature the simple Man of Nazareth has here assumed! He is the mighty judge of the universe, who sits at the right hand of God, at whose coming the sun is darkened, the moon fails to give her light, the stars fall and the powers of heaven are moved. Legions of Angels attend him. At the sound of his trumpet-call the elect gather from the four quarters of the earth. And what a judgment that will be! Let us hear how he himself describes it: "When the Son of Man shall come in his majesty, and all the angels with him, then shall he sit upon the seat of his majesty. And all nations shall be gathered together before him, and he shall separate them one from another, as the shepherd *Matt.* separateth the sheep from the goats! And he shall set the *xxv. 31 ff.* sheep on his right hand, but the goats on his left. Then shall the king say to them that shall be on his right hand: Come, ye blessed of my Father, possess you the kingdom prepared for you from the foundation of the world. . . . Then he shall say to them also that shall be on his left hand: Depart from me, you cursed, into everlasting fire which was prepared for the devil and his angels! What a manifestation! What verdicts! What majesty in the judge! Jesus applies to himself Daniel's title of Son of Man, but his claim penetrates beyond the clouds of heaven even to the right hand of God.

In the first chapter of the Apocalypse we find the mighty vision of the Son of Man. "I was in the spirit on the Lord's day, and I heard behind me a great voice, as of a trumpet . . . and I turned to see the voice that spoke with me. And being turned, I saw seven golden candlesticks, and in the midst of the seven golden candlesticks, one like to the Son of Man, clothed with a garment down to the feet, and girt with a golden girdle. And his head and his hairs were white as white wool, and as snow, and his eyes were as a flame of fire. And his feet like unto fine brass, as in a burning furnace. And his voice as the sound of many waters. And he had in his right hand seven stars. And from his mouth came out a sharp two-edged sword, and his face was as the sun shineth in his power." A vision, a mere picture it was that John saw and portrayed in these words, but a picture so fraught with living strength and awful power and compelling majesty that the seer "fell at his feet as dead." But at the last judgment it will be no mere vision that will appear in the clouds of heaven, but the judging God in the form and figure of the man of Nazareth. And the glorious vision of the Apocalypse will fade into nothingness before the terrible grandeur of the reality.

Apoc. i. 10ff.

But the Man Jesus will not wait until the end of time to assume the role of judge. His tribunal is already sitting: his judgment is already in progress. He himself has said so: "Now is the judgment of the world: now shall the prince of this world be cast out." In all times and for all men his figure and message act as a permanent tribunal in which final and irrevocable decisions are made. "This child is set for the fall, and for the resurrection of many in Israel and for a sign which shall be contradicted." By contact with him will "the thoughts of many hearts become revealed." "He is the stone which was rejected by the builders, which is become the head of the corner." He is the omniscient One, who, to his Church, to every people, to each individual soul may say: "I know thy works."

John xii. 31

Luke ii. 34f.

Acts iv. 11
Apoc. i. 2

However, Jesus is not by any means Son of Man only in view of the great judgment he must carry out. As Son of Man he is redeemer as well as judge, and he repeatedly refers to himself as Son of Man when speaking of his redemptive role. "The Son of Man is come to seek and to save that which was lost." "The Son of Man is not come to be ministered unto, but to minister, and to give his life a redemption for many." He it is who sets the good seed, and who, as Lord even of the Sabbath, sets aside the law of the Jews, and who assumes to himself authority to forgive sins on earth in his own name. From the sublime heights of his merciful Redeemer-hood he issues to weary mankind his invitation to "come to me, all you that labour and are burdened, and I will refresh you." And he knows himself to be one with the Divine Wisdom when he continues in a tone almost of supplication: "Take up my yoke upon you, and learn of me, because I am meek, and humble of heart: and you shall find rest to your souls, for my yoke is sweet, and my burden light."

Luke xix. 10

Matt. xx. 28

Matt. xi. 26

In complete submission to his Father's command he was ready to crown his redemptive work by total surrender in suffering and death. Three times he foretold to his Apostles his approaching Passion and Death, and each time he predicates it of the Son of Man. "The Son of Man must suffer many things: and be rejected by the ancients and chief priests and scribes, and be killed, and the third day rise again." And again "while they all wondered at the things he did, he said to his disciples: "Lay you up in your hearts these words, for it shall come to pass that the Son of Man shall be delivered into the hands of men." And further on St. Luke tells us that "Jesus took unto him the twelve, and said to them: Behold we go up to Jerusalem, and all things shall be accomplished which were written by the prophets con-

Luke ix. 22ff.

cerning the Son of Man. For he shall be delivered to the
Gentiles, and shall be mocked, and scourged, and spit
upon; and after they have scourged him, they will put
him to death; and the third day he shall rise again."

Luke xviii. 31 ff.

Thus did the Man Jesus embody in one person as Son
of Man the double character of redeemer and judge,
and in this two-fold role we must especially study him,
for here he takes on unmistakable characteristics of
Jahve, the Old Testament revelation of God, who, in the
psalms, and by the prophets and historians of Israel is
portrayed primarily in this dual role. Then they break
forth into impassioned words. They see the "Lord"
throned in divine majesty as he delivers judgment from
his judgment seat. "He shall judge the world in equity,
he shall judge the people in justice." Soon the avenging
God is invoked in ringing tones: "Lift up thyself, thou
that judgest the earth; render a reward to the proud";
and again the psalmist plunges into a description of the
judicial coming of the Most High, and rejoices at the
annihilation of the enemy: "Clouds and darkness are
round about him: justice and judgement are the establishment of his throne. A fire shall go before him, and
shall burn his enemies round about. His lightnings have
shone forth to the world: the earth saw and trembled.
The mountains melted like wax at the presence of the
Lord: at the presence of the Lord of all the earth. The
heavens declared his justice; and all people saw his
glory." Woe to him on whom the divine judge pours
forth the vials of his wrath!

Ps. ix. 8 ff.

Ps. xciii. 1 ff.

Ps. xcvi. 2 ff.

But this avenging, judging, terrible God is also the
God who is close to us, the object of our hope and love,
the one sure help in every need. Side by side with the
idea of God as judge there runs through the Old Testament picture the predominant idea of Him as the object
of our love and trust. This mentality is not founded on

the universal creature-creator relationship but on the relationship of grace, the bond between God and his people. What tender tones the inspired writers adopt when they depict the forgiving and redeeming God. Let us take a passage at random. In the 54th chapter of the Book of Isaias we read: "Fear not, for thou shalt not be confounded . . . he that made thee shall rule over thee . . . the Lord of Hosts is his name . . ., and thy Redeemer, the Holy One of Israel, shall be called the God of all the earth. . . . For a moment have I forsaken thee, but with great mercies will I gather thee. . . . Depart far from oppression, for thou shalt not fear; and from terror, for it shall not come near thee."

Isaias liv. 4ff.

The Old Testament revelation of God, then, is based essentially on the relationship of judge-redeemer. It is difficult to say which characteristic is the more predominant, and hence to a certain extent the divine portrait remains indeterminate.

God the Redeemer is the unapproachable divine Majesty. But this unapproachable and Holy One is the absolutely just, good, true and trustworthy one. His splendor and superiority do not repel and terrify us; rather do they summon us to joy, hope and boundless love.

Have we not therein likewise portrayed for us the impression which radiated from the Son of Man? In him also we find exemplified the judge-redeemer role. His portrait too remains indefinite, but in it we may clearly see the Redeemer and the Judge. He who ignores one of these characteristics, or emphasizes one to the exclusion of the other, falsifies the whole picture. He robs Christ of his severity or his goodness, both of which are essential elements to the beauty of his manly fatherly character.

4. THE ONLY-BEGOTTEN SON OF GOD

During his Galilean mission Jesus once came into the region of Caesarea-Philippi. He was alone with his Apostles, and in a retrospective mood he cast a glance back over his work, and put to the twelve the question: "Whom do men say that the Son of Man is?" They answered: "Some John the Baptist, and others Elias, and others Jeremias, or one of the prophets: Jesus saith to them: But whom do you say that I am? Simon Peter answered and said: Thou art Christ the Son of the living God. And Jesus answering, said to him: Blessed art thou, Simon Bar-Jona, because flesh and blood hath not revealed it to thee, but my Father who is in heaven." Whereupon he made Peter the foundation stone of the Church.

Matt. xvi. 13ff.

In the words quoted above Peter makes his profession of faith in a statement solemnly made by Jesus on a previous occasion. "All things are delivered to me by my Father. And no one knoweth the Son but the Father, neither doth any one know the Father, but the Son, and he to whom it shall please the Son to reveal Him." This declaration naturally reached the ears of the Sanhedrin and they were highly scandalized. When Jesus stood on trial before judge and accusers Caiphas said to him: "I adjure thee by the living God, that thou tell us if thou be the Christ the Son of God." Jesus answered: "Thou hast said it. Nevertheless I say to you, hereafter you shall see the Son of Man sitting on the right hand of the power of God, and coming in the clouds of heaven." There was no withdrawal or modifying of his claim; he would be known as the Son of God in the sense in which he had used it all his life. And the high priest understood and appreciated the tremendous earnestness of the declaration, for he "rent his garments" saying: "He hath blasphemed, what further need have we of witnesses?

Matt. xi. 27

Matt. xxvi. 63ff.

And they answering said: He is guilty of death." He had claimed to be God, so he was condemned to death for blasphemy.

But Jesus stood by his declaration in spite of the consequences. He could not, and dared not, give himself out to be less than he actually was: the Messias and real Son of God. His was a twofold life: a pre-worldly, eternal life in his Divine Nature, and an earthly, temporal life in his human nature. He was at once God and man.

Why did Jesus insist on calling himself the Son of God rather than simply God? By so doing he afforded us a glance into the inner life of the Godhead. To him we owe the revelation of the Holy Trinity, and the knowledge that in God there are the three Divine Persons, Father, Son and Holy Ghost, each possessing in full one and the same Divine Nature, but each in his own way. The Father possesses it from all eternity. He has received it from none other than himself, but he is also the origin of the divine nature in the other two persons. "The origin of the whole Godhead," He has been designated by a Council of the Church. The Son receives it from the Father alone by an eternal spiritual generation. The Holy Ghost receives it from Father and Son alike as by a common breathing. In some such infinitely inadequate manner we attempt to describe in human language that mysterious procession which passes the bounds of human comprehension. Christ, therefore, describes himself as Son of God precisely because that is what he was and is, having been begotten by the Father from all eternity. Already in the second psalm the psalmist causes the kingly Messias to declare himself: "The Lord hath said to me: Thou art my Son; this day (i.e. in the eternal Now, from eternity) have I begotten thee." *Psalms ii. 7*

The fact that in God there is a real, if thoroughly spiritual, generation is the subject of an article of faith,

but there is no explanation why the fruit of this generation is universally accepted as male. The reference is to a
Son, and not merely to a child, and certainly there is no
question of a daughter. God is a spirit. There can be no
reference to him in terms of the corporal and sexual; that
is merely a way of expressing to ourselves in human
language the immaterial and inexpressible. Bearing this
in mind, let us then ask ourselves why the sources of
revelation speak exclusively of a Son in God. Why do
they ascribe to the second Person of the Godhead so
definitely and universally a masculine nature?

The Divine Image of supernatural revelation mani-
fests decidedly masculine characteristics. In it there is
nothing of a vague, nondescript deity, or of indefinite,
indeterminate, neutral natural powers; it depicts a personal God, the embodiment of living power and strength.

He is simply the Lord. The predominant distinguishing marks of His being are His powers of creation and
life-giving, of fashioning and preserving, of guiding and
directing. Thus Job describes him in his reply to his
friends: "With him is wisdom and strength: he hath
Job counsel and understanding." And the prophet Isaias
xii. 13, 16 testifies of Him: "Lift up your eyes on high, and see who
hath created these things, who bringeth out their host by
number and calleth them all by their names. By the
greatness of his might and strength and power, not one
Isaias of them was missing." Moses entreats him: "Lord God,
xi. 26 thou hast begun to show unto thy servant thy greatness,
and most mighty hand; for there is no other God either
in heaven or earth, that is able to do thy works, to be
Deut. compared to thy strength." But neither psalmist nor
iii. 24 prophets can find words adequate to describe the power
and strength of God's dominion, and His creative and
formative activity in the world of men and matter. And
when chosen souls attempt to express the experiences they

have had in their intercourse with God, they, in common with all the sources of revelation, attribute to Him masculine characteristics.

Now the second person of the Godhead is always depicted as the image and likeness of the first person. The fruit of the Divine generation bears such a perfect resemblance to His Begetter that we must speak of identity of essence in both, and if the Begetter is conceived as masculine, that must hold also for the Begotten. This fruit, indentical in essence with the Father, can be none other than the only Son, for only a Son can resemble his father in everything.

Jesus of Nazareth, therefore, in his pre-worldly existence, even before his Incarnation, was already the Son of God. He is never referred to in the Scriptures as "child" of God, as we are described as by grace the adopted children of God. And while the Apostle Paul in his letters refers to Christians in general as "sons" of God, and attributes "sonship" to them, St. John, on the other hand, in his writings reserves the title "Son" exclusively for Christ, and refers to Christians as "children of God." In the New Testament, when the word "son" is used it is always in reference to the only Son of God, and when it is intended to emphasize the unique traits of the second Divine Person the portrait drawn is always that of a virile young man.

We must elaborate further. The evangelist describes the Son of God as the "only begotten": "The Word was made flesh, and dwelt amongst us, and we saw his glory, the glory as it were of the only-begotten of the Father full of grace and truth." "No man hath seen God at any time: the only-begotten Son who is in the bosom of the Father, he hath declared him." "By this hath the charity of God appeared towards us, because God hath sent his only-begotten Son into the world, that we may live by *John i. 14*

John v. 15

*John
i. iv. 9*

him." The "only-begotten" stands in a unique, incomparable relationship to the Father, and in him the Father empties Himself of His infinite love, since He had no other Son to share it. And so St. John dares to plead it as the highest and greatest proof of God's love for us that he gave "his only-begotten Son." In the Old Testa-

*John
iii. 16*

ment the "only-begotten" is not infrequently referred to simply as the "beloved Son," and this was likewise the expression used by the heavenly voice giving testimony of

*Matt.
iii. 17
Rom.
viii. 29
I Col.
xv. 18*

Jesus at his baptism: "This is my beloved Son, in whom I am well pleased." Paul calls him "the first-born amongst many brethren," "the first-born of every creature," "the first-born from the dead."

The first-born and only-begotten is always the father's pride and joy. He inherits the father's vitality in all its pristine vigor. Among many peoples the first-born enjoys many privileges not shared by the other members of the family. In ancient Israel he had a special claim to his father's blessing, and received a double share of the paternal heritage. Therefore he must be considered as first and fairest flower and vigorous fruit of the unshared and unimpaired virility of the father.

All that is included in the expression "only-begotten Son of God." All the infinite abundance of the life and power of God was transmitted to him. All that nature can possibly bestow of temporal gifts we must consider his: the tenderness of budding childhood, the charm of blossoming youth, the ripe maturity of manhood. Each moment he is born anew, and as old as eternity. In him there is no growing old, and no diminution of strength.

As the only-begotten Son he is the unique confidant of the Father. Him alone the Father initiates into his deep, eternal secrets. "No one knoweth the Father, but the

*Matt.
xi. 27*

Son, and he to whom it shall please the Son to reveal him." The Father is in him, and he in the Father; theirs

is a perfect communion of life and essence. All that is the
Father's is his; all that is his is likewise the Father's.
What the Father does, the Son does equally. As the
Father has life in Himself, so he has given to the Son to
have life in himself. As the Father works until this hour,
so the Son works. He is the creative co-worker with the
Father, and like Him, the possessor of divine power and
strength, the bearer and awakener of life.

Everywhere in revelation the second person in God is
described as the "only-begotten" and "first-born," the
virile, powerful Son of the Father, the "likeness of His
Being and the brightness of His Glory." The noblest
images and boldest representations are drawn from the
sphere of masculine and youthful life in the effort to
depict for us the splendor and life which the Son enjoyed in the bosom of the Father even before the world
was. And all these images and comparisons emphasize
his manliness, strength, might and creative power. The
incomparable splendor of Divine manhood rests on
him, even before he makes his visible appearance in the
world of men.

But it is only when he is portrayed as future Messianic
king that his person radiates the full glory of his manhood. The prophet Isaias boasts of him: "Government
is upon his shoulder. His name shall be called Wonder-
ful, Counsellor, God the Mighty. . . . He shall sit upon
the throne of David, and upon his kingdom . . . The *Isaias*
Spirit of the Lord shall rest upon him . . . the spirit of *ix. 5ff.*
counsel and fortitude. . . . He shall strike the earth *xi. 2*
with the rod of his mouth, and with the breath of his lips
he shall stay the wicked."

The second psalm sings of the victory of the Messianic
king over the enemies of God. God Himself has called
him and anointed him king of His Divine kingdom: "I
have appointed him king over Sion, my holy mountain."

And the Messias himself is introduced to us: "The Lord hath said to me: Thou art my Son; this day have I begotten thee. Ask of me, and I will give thee the Gentiles for thy inheritance, and the utmost parts of the earth for thy possession. Thou shalt rule them with a rod of iron, and shalt break them in pieces like a potter's vessel." Similarly in Psalm 109 the Messias is depicted as the mighty and victorious king called by God. But it is in Psalm 44 that the singer is completely transported by the beauty of the heavenly bridegroom, and must *Psalm* perforce break forth into ecstatic song of praise: "Thou *xliv. 3ff.* art beautiful above the sons of men: grace is poured abroad in thy lips: therefore hath God blessed thee forever. . . . With thy comeliness and thy beauty set out, proceed prosperously and reign."

Just as in the Psalms and prophetic utterances the figure of the future Messianic king is the center of attraction, the Apocalypse is built around the risen Christ who is appointed judge of the world. The whole structure of the book circles specially around his person. We have already spoken of the portrait of the son of man in the introductory vision. In the fifth chapter he appears as "the lion of the tribe of Judea, the root of David." He alone can open the book with seven seals. He stands as Judge and Master at the central point of the history of mankind; he is man's creative beginning and interior goal!

And then the picture changes. The lamb stands before us "as it were slain," and yet full of strength and life. That is testified by its "seven horns and seven eyes," for in scripture the horn is the symbol of strength, while the number seven stands for perfection and abundance.

But the most thrilling picture of all is that of the rider on the horse which we find in Chapter 19. "I saw heaven opened, and behold a white horse: and he that sat upon him was called Faithful and True, and with justice doth he judge and fight. And his eyes were as a flame of fire, and on his head were many diadems, and he had a name written, which no man knoweth but himself. And he was clothed with a garment sprinkled with blood: and his name is called The Word of God. . . . And he hath on his garments and on his thigh written: King of Kings and Lord of Lords."

Let us now turn once again to the man of Nazareth. If we allow all the powerful descriptions and splendid pictures which were penned of him, both before and after his visible appearance in the world, to work upon us, we must perforce become aware of the ardent fire that burnt in this heart. What kind of man was that! One wonders why this mean, insignificant, limited nature of ours was not burst asunder by the abundance of power and dignity, of life and strength, of wealth and splendor which operated within him. For the eternal Son of God and the poor carpenter of Nazareth were one single personality, one single central point of thought and feeling, one unique radiance of unlimited power and activity. A man walked this earth, a man with veiled countenance, as of old that of Moses when he returned from Mount Sinai. But the dazzling light of this man's brightness breaks through the veil.

This incomparable manhood was, indeed, fashioned and perfected by the Godhead; nevertheless the human character of the earthly man formatively influences the portrait of his Divinity.

5. THE WORD OF GOD

"God, who, at sundry times and in divers manners, spoke in times past to the fathers by the prophets, last of all in these days hath spoken to us by His Son." These words of introduction to the Epistle to the Hebrews contain a short summary of the history of supernatural revelation. God's revelation of the salvation of mankind reached its climax and conclusion in and through Jesus Christ. Through him was achieved the deepest and richest revelation. He was the greatest of all the prophets.

But he was much more. To see in him merely a prophet, even if the most significant of all the prophets, is to fail to recognize the salient and decisive thing in his person. To be a prophet means to be an instrument of God's revelation, a proclaimer of God's word. In and by Jesus Christ the Word of God was proclaimed to the world in a unique and final way; he was unparalleled among the prophets. For they were ordinary men, chosen by God and entrusted with a divine mission. One day "the word of God came to them," as we read in the introduction to most of the prophetical books. Or else it is a "vision," a "manifestation," a "prophecy," an "utterance" which they received from God to pass on to men. St. Luke relates of the old man, Simeon: "He hath received an answer from the Holy Ghost, that he should not see death before he had seen the Christ of the Lord." And of John the Baptist we read: "The word of the Lord was made unto John, the son of Zachary in the desert."

Such statements are never made of Jesus. Nowhere do we read that any single manifestation came to him. Doubtless the evangelists avoided this manner of speaking because they felt it would be unseemly and insufficient when referring to Christ; it would not be in accordance with the mysterious relationship he bore to God. A man who dares to assert of himself: "All things are delivered to me by my Father. And no one knoweth the Son but the Father: neither doth any one know the Father but the Son, and he to whom it shall please the Son to reveal him" is not merely the recipient of the

Matt. xi. 27

Godhead, he rather stands permanently therein, and speaks out of a hitherto unheard-of fullness and depth of knowledge of the things of God. Jesus praises the Father, the Lord of Heaven and earth, because he "hath revealed it to little ones"; he congratulates Peter on his having received his knowledge of the Messias from the Father in Heaven, but we never hear him give thanks to God for a revelation he himself has received. The prophets often received a call to their prophetic work in a striking manner, but there is nothing sensational about the call of Jesus. The beginning of his public activity is chronicled for us in words of unadorned, almost startling, simplicity; "Then cometh Jesus from Galilee to the Jordan, unto John," or "From that time Jesus began to preach." The occurrence which took place at his Baptism in the Jordan was not so much a calling as a manifestation of his Person.

Matt. xi. 25

Matt. iii. 13 iv. 17

In proof of the statement that the evangelists avoided placing Jesus on a level with the other messengers of God is the fact that they very rarely say of him that he preached the "word of God," or proclaimed the "Word." Matthew never uses this turn of speech, though it does occur a few times in St. Mark, St. Luke, and the Acts of the Apostles. As regards the manner of speaking, the person of Jesus acts like a magnetic force on the expressions "word" and "Word of God." Again and again they are drawn within the charmed circle of his person, and his activity, again and again caught up by him, ever more exclusively applied to him until he has, so to speak, won the monopoly of them, until his person simply becomes identified with them.

In the Old Testament a single divine communication, or the sum of the revelations and pronouncements made to a prophet were equally designated the Word of God. The Old Law, the sum of God's redemptive dealings with men, was summed up under this name. In the New Testament writings we find citations from the Old Testament interpreted as the Word of God; indeed, the whole gamut of God's work for the salvation of man, the supernatural Revelation in the Old and New Testaments comes under this name.

But since the appearance of Jesus Christ the expressions "Word" and "Word of God" in Scripture are used exclusively to denote his person and his work, so that when the terms are now employed they are immediately and universally interpreted as the Gospel, its pronouncements and the events connected with his person. This "word" is not merely preached; it "happens." It is not merely "heard," "received" or "rejected"; it "increases," "works," "propagates itself" or otherwise works out a destiny. And "service in the Word" denotes the sum of one's efforts in the service of the things of Jesus Christ.

But this relating of the "Word" and "Word of God" to the person of Jesus Christ can be carried a step further. As Jesus not only has shown the way, but is himself the Way, not only has preached the truth but is himself the Truth, not only has communicated life but is himself Life, so likewise he has not merely preached the "Word" and "Word of God," but he is himself this Word of God. St. John boldly develops this identification, for as Paul *I Cor.* speaks of "Christ Jesus, who of God is made unto us *i. 30* wisdom, and justice, and sanctification, and redemption," John says of him that he has become the "Word" *Eph.* for us. For as he is our "Peace," he is equally the *ii. 14* "Word." We can almost see John as he pens the vivid prologue to his first epistle: "That which was from the beginning, which we have heard, which we have seen with our own eyes, which we have looked upon, and our hands have handled, of the Word of life . . . we declare unto you." His manner of writing, his short staccato

phrases, show that he is wrestling with the inherent difficulty of his subject, the difficulty of expressing the inexpressible. In the introduction to his Gospel he clearly
identifies Christ with the Word, and he gives the reader
no clue as to how he is to interpret the "Word" because
he presumes that this is already known. Nor does he give
the reader of the Apocalyptic vision of the rider on the
white horse any other interpretation than: "his name is
called the Word of God," that Word, he would say, that
is known to you all.

For our purpose it is of supreme importance and significance to note what attributes were ascribed to the
Word of God in the Old Testament. All the prophets
emphasize the dynamic character of the Word; it is
tremendously effective, creative and energetic; it is a
heavenly power which faithfully accomplishes its task on
earth; it is a Word to which clings a striking acuteness
and keenness, a Word which is a blessing to him who
accepts it, but which will prove a two-edged sword for
the confusion and destruction of him who resists it. It
was the prophet Jeremias who perceived most clearly the
dynamic quality of the Word of God. To him it is "a
reproach and a derision," and at the same time his joy
and gladness. It is light and truth, which unmasks the
hypocrite and relentlessly exposes his spiritual poverty.
To the prophet Amos it is a vital power without which
man cannot exist, and Isaias tells us that to those who are
obdurate of heart the Word will be a sentence of destruction.

Jesus Christ is the living embodiment of the Word of
God. He is the personification of all those attributes
which the Scriptures predicate of this Word. His power
was obvious to all. He was goodness and mildness itself,
and in all his works he manifested the love of God for
mankind. "He went about doing good," St. Peter tells *Acts*
x. 38

us. He forced nobody, avoided noisy propaganda for his object, did not behave like a conquering invader, killing and laying waste as he went, nor did he fume and rage like an angry nature-god. And yet he is the Word of God which judges, exhorts, decides and demands decisions. He is the keen-edged sword, and he is come not to send peace upon earth but the sword, to set father against son, and mother against daughter. The bruised reed he will *Matt.* not break, nor will he extinguish the smoking flax, but *x. 34–39* yet he warns us that if we would find life we must first lose it for his sake.

Did this living, vigorous Word not strike as a lightning flash into that Jerusalem where he scourged the buyers and sellers out of the holy house of God? Did it not burst forth as a destroying judgment as he uttered his last warning to the obstinate Scribes and Pharisees? As the eternal Word of God he reveals himself when he utters the words: "Heaven and earth shall pass away, but my words shall not pass away." His prayers at the Last Supper: "Father, I have finished the work which Thou gavest me to do," and his last cry on the cross: "It is consummated" resound like a grand "Amen" to the declaration spoken by God through the mouth of the *Isaias* prophet Isaias: "My Word which shall go forth from *lv. 10, 11* my mouth shall not return to me void, but it shall do whatsoever I please, and shall prosper in the things for which I sent it."

The Man Jesus was the Word of God. Could his manhood be better depicted than in attributing to him all the qualities which the Holy Scripture predicates of the Word of God? Did he not smite the hearts of men as a two-edged sword, at once judging and healing? Did he not come "to cast fire on the earth"? Has his hammer not broken rocks to pieces? Did this Word not strike as a lightning-flash into the very soul of mankind? What a false character-sketch of Christ we should produce, were we to deny or keep silence about his sharpness and severity! To represent the sharp sword as a graceful shepherd's staff, the flaming fire as a tepid glow, the destroying hammer as a soft handshake, and the descending lightning-flash as a flickering candle-flame would be a complete falsification of the person of the Messias. Such as that the Man Jesus was not. Such as that was not the Word that God spoke to men.

The whole Man Jesus, all his thinking and willing, his speaking and doing was a revelation. It was the Word of God. All the fullness of the holiness and power and love of God lived in this man. His character is identical with that of the Word. There was only one such man. Only once did God speak this Word, but the Word that He spoke remains for all eternity.

A NOTE ON THE TYPE

IN WHICH THIS BOOK IS SET

This book is set in Baskerville, an Intertype face, created from the original types used by John Baskerville, the eighteenth-century typefounder and printer. This type has long been considered one of the finest book types ever developed. The letters are wide and open and have a businesslike approach. The finer hairlines give exquisite delicacy. The heavier strokes give color and strength. The relation of the two in combination gives a brilliant effect and makes for easy reading. The book was composed and printed by the York Composition Company, Inc. of York, Pa., and bound by Moore and Company of Baltimore. The typography and design are by Howard N. King.